Frog

Animal
Series editor: Jonathan Burt

Already published

Ant Charlotte Sleigh · *Ape* John Sorenson · *Bear* Robert E. Bieder
Bee Claire Preston · *Camel* Robert Irwin · *Cat* Katharine M. Rogers
Chicken Annie Potts · *Cockroach* Marion Copeland · *Cow* Hannah Velten
Crow Boria Sax · *Dog* Susan McHugh · *Donkey* Jill Bough
Duck Victoria de Rijke · *Eel* Richard Schweid · *Elephant* Daniel Wylie
Falcon Helen Macdonald · *Fly* Steven Connor · *Fox* Martin Wallen
Frog Charlotte Sleigh · *Giraffe* Mark Williams · *Hare* Simon Carnell
Horse Elaine Walker · *Hyena* Mikita Brottman · *Kangaroo* John Simons
Lion Deirdre Jackson · *Lobster* Richard J. King · *Moose* Kevin Jackson
Mosquito Richard Jones · *Otter* Daniel Allen · *Owl* Desmond Morris
Oyster Rebecca Stott · *Parrot* Paul Carter · *Peacock* Christine E. Jackson
Penguin Stephen Martin · *Pig* Brett Mizelle · *Pigeon* Barbara Allen
Rat Jonathan Burt · *Rhinoceros* Kelly Enright · *Salmon* Peter Coates
Shark Dean Crawford · *Snail* Peter Williams · *Snake* Drake Stutesman
Sparrow Kim Todd · *Spider* Katja and Sergiusz Michalski · *Swan* Peter Young
Tiger Susie Green · *Tortoise* Peter Young · *Trout* James Owen
Vulture Thom Van Dooren · *Whale* Joe Roman · *Wolf* Garry Marvin

Frog

Charlotte Sleigh

REAKTION BOOKS

For Nick, who has no need of metamorphosing,
thank you very much

Published by
REAKTION BOOKS LTD
33 Great Sutton Street
London EC1V ODX, UK
www.reaktionbooks.co.uk

First published 2012
Copyright © Charlotte Sleigh 2012

Printed and bound in China by C&C Offset Printing Co., Ltd

British Library Cataloguing in Publication Data
Sleigh, Charlotte.
    Frog. – (Animal)
    1. Frogs 2. Frogs in literature.
    3. Frogs as laboratory animals.
    4. Frogs in art.
    I. Title II. Series
    597.8'9-DC23

ISBN 978 1 86189 920 0

Contents

Introduction

Frogs are slippery in more ways than one.

Above all, they are liminal creatures: animals of the in-between. They are the largest creatures to undergo such complete and dramatic metamorphosis, transforming from an aquatic to a terrestrial existence in the process. Even as adults many species are still partially creatures of the water, but they are not formed like other aquatic vertebrates. Apart from their close cousins the newts, frogs are the only underwater swimmers with legs; they are also among the very few vertebrates not to possess tails. Add these features to their front-facing eyes, their slim waists and hairless bodies, and you have a beast that is curiously human in form.

It was perhaps the doubtful nature of frogs that led the natural historian Ulisse Aldrovandi (1522–1605) to include them so prominently in his museum of curiosities and monsters: a frog with the tail of a lizard, and another with a full set of teeth carefully planted inside its mouth. Cabinets such as Aldrovandi's were a part of the Renaissance drive to order nature, and frogs have remained a problematic grouping ever since, as liminal in their classification as in their biology. A classroom study conducted in New Zealand found that the frog was not even necessarily an animal. Only about half of fifteen-year-olds classed it as such; for the rest, animality was tacitly associated

ADMIRANDA
LEVIVM SPECTACVLA
RERVM

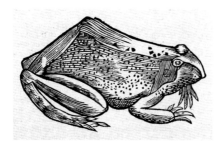

Like other early moderns, Edward Topsell classified frogs with snakes in his *History of Serpents* (1608).

with mammalian characteristics. Being furless and aquatic, the frog did not count.[1]

The challenge of frog classification is a particular favourite of anthropologists. An influential paper of 1979 suggested that when non-Westerners develop zoological taxonomies they get to frogs comparatively late in the process and struggle with how to categorize them. The paper's model suggested that there are three basic life forms – FISH, SNAKE and BIRD – that are classified early on in the development of a language. MAMMAL and WUG (worm and bug), it was claimed, follow on later; and frogs, when speakers finally get round to them, have to be crow barred into one of these.[2] However, other studies – largely conducted in New Guinea – have shown that frogs are a lot more significant to forest dwellers than these researchers anticipated, intimately related with each language group's specific ecology, lifestyle and culture. FROG is, in fact, often labelled before MAMMAL or WUG in the development of a language, and the detailed categorizations of frogs produced by New Guineans can be remarkably close to the taxonomies generated by Western scientists.[3]

One could argue that the anthropologists' rather elementary and universalist model for the development of the category FROG in 1979 actually captured their own heritage rather better than that of the New Guineans. The anthropologists' two options for

Frontispiece to August Johan Roesel von Rosenhof, *Historia Naturalis Ranarum Nostratium* (1758). The Latin motto from Virgil translates as 'the greatest wonder may be derived from observation of the slightest things'; the crumbling monument, juxtaposed with vivacious amphibians, reasserts the point in pictorial form.

This undated engraving from the Stuart era underlines the often negative reputation of batrachians. A sinful courtier in Whitehall is compared to a toad and found – astonishingly – to be the more loathsome of the two.

including frogs, WUG and MAMMAL, were both leftover groups: neither FISH, SNAKE nor BIRD. Frogs have long been just such hard-to-fit animals for Europeans, grouped variously with insects and serpents until early modern times. In 1608 Edward Topsell put them with serpents: 'By serpents we understand in this discourse all venomous Beasts, whether creeping without legs . . . or with legs . . . or more nearly compacted bodies, as Toads, Spiders and Bees.'[4]

The frog's appearance in a French dictionary of 1694 saw it defined as 'an insect that commonly lives in marshes'. The great comparative anatomist of the nineteenth century, Georges Cuvier (1769–1832), made the batrachians (frogs and toads) the fourth order of reptiles; the class Reptilia remained the taxonomic home of the frogs until the mid- to late nineteenth century. Batrachians were defined by their deficits in relation to the other reptiles: their lack of fully formed ribs, of scales, of a pharynx, and of external organs of generation.

To this very day the discipline of herpetology – literally, the study of creeping animals – retains the scientific grouping together of reptiles and amphibians in a way that would seem very odd for, say, specialists in birds and mammals. In scientific literature and at academic conferences, frogs continue to sit alongside lizards and snakes. This grouping reflects – even if it no longer shares – a medieval tradition that saw these creatures as imperfect, if not downright satanic. The frog and toad were not so far from the devilish serpent himself.

The category 'frog' is itself subdivided different ways by different cultures. Europeans are consistent in distinguishing frogs and toads, the latter being considered to have drier, wartier skin; to have a flatter profile; and to walk rather than hopping as frogs do. For Topsell, the toad was the 'most noble kinde of Frog, most venomous and remarkable for courage and strength', but in general (and even elsewhere in Topsell's *History of Serpents*) Europeans have regarded toads with more disgust and suspicion than frogs – and have maintained separate words for them.[5] The Germanic root of 'frog' seems to come from an early Indo-European verb meaning 'to hop', while Romance languages trace their frog names to the Latin *rana* (frog). Both

An early modern English *frogge*: detail of hanging embroidered by Mary Queen of Scots and Bess of Hardwick, c. 1570.

Frogs of the genus *Hyla*, from Johann Baptist de Spix's *Animalia Nova sive Species Novae Testudinum et Ranarum* (1824). The genus consists entirely of tree frogs, one of the most widely recognized subcategories of frog around the world.

French and German trace their words for toad to a root referring to their rough skin, although the Latin *bufo* (toad) is related to a Germanic verb meaning 'to puff'. (The English 'toad' is a mysteriously isolated linguistic stump all on its own.) However, the derivation of *rana* complicates the idea of a linguistic separation of frogs and toads. Although sometimes considered to be onomatopoeic, it is more likely a corruption of the Greek *frýnos*, which means 'toad'. In other parts of the world, where both ecology and culture are different, the batrachians break down in different ways. Japanese, for example, has the same root word for both frogs and toads. Other languages have three or even more basic categories, with tree frogs especially often distinguished from marshy frogs.

Current biology gives frogs the status of a taxonomic order, the Anura. The Anura are themselves split three ways into sub-orders that comprise 38 families in all. Every frog is an anuran, and every anuran is a frog. Biologists do not recognize any biological distinction between frogs and toads; most of the anuran families contain within them some species that are informally designated 'frog' and others as 'toad'. Only the family Bufonidae contains 'toads' alone. This book follows scientists' lead in treating all the anurans, frogs and toads, together.

Modern amphibians (anurans, newts and salamanders, and primitive caecilians) seem to have developed from the Temnospondyli, an order of primitive and sometimes gigantic amphibia that lived approximately 250 to 300 million years ago. However, for a long time scientists could not find an intermediate organism, from which modern frogs and salamanders diverged, among the Temnospondyli, and some suggested that a different order altogether was likely to be their point of common ancestry. In 2006 scientists at the University of Calgary claimed to have settled the dispute by finding the frog and salamander's common ancestor in a Texan temnospondyl fossil named *Gerobatrachus hottoni* (Hotton's Old Frog). This 'frogamander' is, at 11.5 cm, about the size of a modern frog. It shares features of both modern-day frogs and salamanders, although at least one specialist in amphibian fossils has cautioned that it may be rather too close to a modern frog to count as a true 'missing link'. *G. hottoni* is about 300 million years old, and if it *is* an ancestor of both salamanders and frogs, then it suggests that the two orders separated about 240 to 275 million years ago. If, as most seem to agree, this is the case, then it leaves another unsolved puzzle, since it represents a much more recent evolutionary divergence than the date suggested by molecular drift (a measure of ancestral similarity that is produced by the DNA-copying errors that accumulate naturally over time). This disagreement will need to be reconciled in some way. Meanwhile, the earliest generally agreed true frog, a partial fossil from Argentina, is roughly 200 million years old. It has been designated as *Vieraella herbsti*, and is very small – about 33 mm from top to rump.

Since the Jurassic period, frogs have colonized most of the Earth. At present over 6,000 extant species are known, slightly more than the maximum (human) capacity of the Albert Hall, or twice that of Carnegie Hall. Around 800 new species have been described in the last five years alone. The only places not inhabited by frogs are the globe's extreme north and south, and the hottest desert areas of Africa and Arabia. Remote oceanic islands are also uncolonized by anurans.

Fossilized frog of the genus *Palaeobatrachus* from the Tertiary period (130–35 million years ago).

The water holding frog (*Litoria platycephala*) of Australia can outlast long periods of drought.

Despite their association with water, anurans are able to live in some remarkably dry environments. The water holding frog, *Litoria platycephala*, inhabits some of the driest and most inhospitable areas of Australia. It survives underground, buried alone with nothing but a bladder full of water to keep it going. In the darkness of the earth it accumulates a cocoon of sloughed-off skin that becomes almost waterproof, reducing the amount of energy that it uses as well as retaining moisture. When rain comes, the frogs emerge to feed and breed. Ideally the rains are an annual event, but if necessary *L. platycephala* can survive inside the earth for up to five years. They lay their eggs in the temporary puddles produced by rain, and like those of other dry-living species, their tadpoles develop very quickly to beat the returning drought. Similarly, spadefoot toads of the southern US (family Scaphiopodidae) have extraordinarily quick development times, as little as seven days from larva to toadlet. No one

A Couch's spadefoot toad (*Scaphiopus couchii*) of the southern US; its extraordinarily quick maturation from tadpole to frog enables it to beat fast-drying conditions.

The North American wood frog (*Rana sylvatica*) survives sub-zero conditions by allowing itself partially to freeze.

knows how the tiny toads migrate and survive the extreme heat of the Californian desert after their puddles disappear.

By contrast, the widely distributed North American wood frog, *Rana sylvatica*, can survive sub-zero temperatures. Its ability to hibernate is nothing special among frogs, but uniquely it is able to tolerate the partial freezing (up to about one-third) of its own body in the process. It uses urea and specially made glucose to reduce the propensity of its body fluid to crystallize, thus protecting its cells from rupture.

Unlike model children, frogs are often heard but not seen. Researchers working with the Karam of the New Guinea Highlands noted that frogs were 'extremely numerous . . . and almost constantly heard' in their environment. In this context, frogs become integral to the human soundscape. When frogs begin to pipe in the evening, the Karam say '*gl agl agp en amnwno*!' – 'when the nyingle-nyangle calls it's time to go home'.[6] Aristophanes exploited the frogs' sound to create a novel chorus in his play of that name. 'Brekekekéx-koáx-koáx' they chant as Dionysus rows across to Hades. The only way Dionysus can deal with his aural irritation is to join in. The nature writer John Burroughs, by contrast, thought the sound a lovely one, auguring the close of winter. 'Blessings on thy warty head:/ No bird could do it better', he concluded in 'The Song of the Toad' (1906).

In many languages, the names of frogs are onomatopoeic: even the English term, when it has its original final syllable restored – frogga – sounds distinctly batrachian. Ouauouarons are Cajun bullfrogs, and Aramaic dialects render frogs as aqruqe or aqruqta; the list of frog-sounding frogs goes on and on.

Frogs almost always make their characteristic species sound – from a peep to a deep burp – for reasons that have to do with reproduction. The commonest of these is the male's call to attract a mate, often performed *en masse*. These calls can be heard up to a mile away; the frog's vocal sac expands like bubblegum to amplify the sound. Other common calls are made with the mouth closed: 'get off!' (when a male is accidentally mounted by another male); 'go away!' (when territory is infringed); and 'eek!' – a distress call emitted when a frog is taken by a predator, and which may possibly startle or distract the latter into letting go.

The order Anura used to be called the Salienta in honour of frogs' other noted characteristic, their capacity to jump. The name was a good one, because even species that have lost the ability (or need) for this form of locomotion retain the morphological features that make it possible. The bones of the hind- and fore legs, separate in other vertebrates, are fused in the frog for extra strength, both in pushing off and in absorbing the shock of landing. The muscles associated with these bones have become hypertrophied through evolution, and ongoing research is exploring the possibility that the tendons are also used like

The Australian rocket frog (*Litoria nasuta*) is named in honour of its projectile power.

BICOLOURED TREE-FROG.—*Phyllomedusa bicolor.*

The giant leaf frog (*Phyllomedusa bicolor*) is among those with the ability to adhere to trees and leaves. The eggs are placed in a leaf nest high above the ground; after 8–10 days the newly hatched tadpoles fall into the pond below. From J. G. Wood's *Illustrated Natural History: Reptiles, Fishes, Molluscs* (1863).

springs to store and release energy for jumping. The Australian rocket frog, *Litoria nasuta*, seems to hold the record in this respect, achieving distances of over two metres. This might not seem so much until one considers that the frog itself is only 5.5 cm long.

Underwater, such leg movements are translated into a kick, generally supplemented by foot webbing that increases push-off against the water. Tree frogs, however, have different requirements, needing to stick to leaves and stems as they make their ascent through the forest canopy. The Australian green tree frog, *Litoria caerulea*, makes the nature of the challenge clear; it is not a tiny, delicate species like so many tree frogs but rather a dumpy and large one, about 10 cm long. Its gravity-defying behaviour is therefore especially in need of explanation. Most tree frogs have a chunky jigsaw of cells on their toe pads which can be wedged into the microscopic chinks of the surface of ascent, a kind of cellular rock-climbing. In addition, frogs produce mucus that sticks their skin to the plant by adhesive molecular forces, just like a wet tissue on glass. Tree frogs constantly reposition their toes to maximize the mucus contact between skin and plant, but – surprisingly – when touched they never feel sticky. Under a powerful microscope the apparently flat cells of *L. caerulea* are revealed to be covered in tightly packed 'nanopillars', each with a small dimple in the end. No one yet knows the exact function of the nanopillars, but they may increase the surface area for adhesion and provide friction against slippage.

Besides the whole-body jump, the other famously fast part of the frog is the tongue, flipping dramatically out of its mouth to capture a passing fly while the frog itself sits in nonchalant immobility. Different species use different mechanisms to pull the trick off. Some actually shorten their tongue as it is protracted, while others lengthen it through the inertial or muscular forces associated with the uncoiling action. Unlike other species which unfurl their tongues, the African pig-nosed frog, *Hemisus marmoratus*, telescopes its tongue outwards, doubling its length in the process. Lobes on the tongue's tip grip the prey in prehensile fashion.

The frog's tongue grabs insects and other invertebrates. Larger species will also take eggs, small vertebrates and even other frogs; only a very small handful of frogs are herbivorous. Tadpoles, on the other hand, have complex mouthparts to allow their specialist filter-feeding on algae. Some tadpoles are also cannibalistic, and contrary to what one might imagine it is often the faster developers that get gobbled up by those still in the larval stage.

An illustration of the frog's fast tongue in action, from Roesel von Rosenhof's *Historia Naturalis Ranarum Nostratium* (1758).

Tadpoles, as is well-known, have gills to breathe as they develop. Adult frogs have very simple lungs, with no diaphragm or rib attachment of pulmonary muscles to assist their intake of air. One species, *Barbourula kalimantanensis*, does without lungs altogether, breathing entirely as other species do partly: through its skin. In order to absorb oxygen, frogs' skin must be kept moist; as an unavoidable side effect it is permeable to many other molecules and must be kept away from salts. Yet despite their inefficient uptake of oxygen, frogs are lively and energetic creatures, qualities that usually depend upon having a lot of oxygen to burn. They manage this by having a strict separation of oxygenated and deoxygenated blood in the heart and around the body, so that what oxygen they do have does not simply diffuse away to oxygen-poor tissue.

The Australian green tree frog (*Litoria caerulea*) is one of many frogs from which pharmacologically active compounds have been obtained – in this case, thanks to a vomiting cat.

The poisonous Southern Corroboree frog (*Pseudophryne corroboree*) is one of the most endangered native animals in Australia.

The most potent of all known toxic frogs: the golden poison frog (*Phyllobates terribilis*) of Colombia.

The skin of different frog species also contains a vast range of pharmacologically significant compounds, whether manufactured by the frogs themselves or ingested in their diet (the scientific jury is still out). The family Bufonidae manufactures poison in the parotoid glands just beneath the eyes, but most frogs produce their chemicals in smaller glands distributed across their backs. Since the 1960s there has been a scientific rush to find, understand, synthesize and patent these compounds. One of the earliest scientific investigations on batrachian pharmacology was prompted by a cat. Robert Endean, an expert on the toxins of marine organisms, noticed that his cat enjoyed eating frogs but always vomited after eating the species *Litoria caerulea*. After extracting the relevant compound from dried frogs' skins, it was found to be a polypeptide that could produce a significant and sustained fall in blood pressure, but unfortunately, as the cat could have told them, it also had the side effect of producing vomiting and diarrhoea. The team named the compound caerulein for the frog; science has not recorded the name of the cat. Caerulein is now used to stimulate gut activity where this property has been damaged, and there are also moves afoot to use it in the treatment of schizophrenia, since a related compound appears to be involved in the neurochemistry

of anxiety. Other frog compounds under investigation include antibiotics, hallucinogens, anti-tumour agents, anti-inflammatories, analgesics, adhesives, spermicides and mosquito repellents. These days, scientists are able to extract these chemicals without killing the frog. Instead, electricity is used to stimulate secretion, but the rarity of many of the species involved makes even their temporary capture an ethically problematic action.

Coloured frogs typically advertise (or in a few cases, bluff) their poisonous properties so that predators leave them alone.

Alas for the frogs, however, some predators have developed tolerance of even their worst weaponry. Humans are not among these tough predators, and members of the family Dendrobatidae of Central and South America are collectively known as poison dart frogs for their use by indigenous peoples. Of these, the golden poison frog, *Phyllobates terribilis*, is the most toxic. It is enough for the Chocó and Cofán Colombians to rub their dart tips against the animal's skin to co-opt its neurotoxic properties to lethal effect, stopping the heart of their victim. It has been estimated that the chemicals contained within a single frog would be enough to kill ten adult humans, but the toxin may also have potential as a topical painkiller if used correctly.

It has served Colombian indigenes well to know of their batrachian neighbours' toxicity, and frogs are in fact generally well-understood around the world. Their metamorphic life cycle is known by most, perhaps all, cultures that are in contact with them. Tadpoles often have affectionate names of their own; in the US and to a lesser extent the UK they are known as pollywogs (or head-wiggles).

The frog's existence is most precarious at the tadpole stage of life. Defenceless and comparatively slow-moving, it, along with its swarm of siblings, is easily hoovered up by predators. Accordingly, frogs have evolved a variety of methods to try and better the chances of their offspring. One of these is sheer numbers: the more tadpoles, the greater the chance of one surviving to replace its parent. However, many species have instead evolved specialist care behaviours in both male and female parents. Females of the now-extinct gastric-brooding frogs of Australia (genus *Rheobatrachus*) managed to suppress the motions and digestive fluids of their stomachs, swallowing their tadpoles and allowing them to develop inside until they were ready to be spat out. The Chilean Darwin's frog (*Rhinoderma*

Another species of highly toxic frog: the dyeing dart frog, *Dendrobates tinctorius* of north-eastern South America. This blue morph was previously thought to be a species in its own right, but *D. tinctorius* is now agreed to be polymorphous (having more than one colour variant).

darwinii) performs a similar feat using its vocal sac. The male 'eats' the eggs when they are close to hatching, and keeps them in the sac for up to 70 days, nourishing them with viscous secretions. Other species develop sacs in the skin along their side or back in which to shelter their young. The fully aquatic Surinam toad (*Pipa pipa*), for example, performs a whirling dance of copulation in the water so that the male can press the fertilized eggs into the female's back. Here they sink into the skin, emerging three to four months later as toadlets. Male toads of the genus *Alytes* do not sacrifice their complexion in this way, but tangle the egg strings around their feet and take regular dips to keep them moist.

Many species will transport their young to good, watery locations, either because the area is otherwise dry and water-transient, or because it is advantageous to find a pool with no predators present. In the latter case, the pool (typically a pocket of water inside a plant) is also free of nutrients for the tadpole, and so food must be provided. The strawberry poison frog (*Dendrobates pumilio*) of Central America is one species that

A Lehmann's poison frog (*Dendrobates lehmanni*) at Cali Zoo, Valle del Cauca, Colombia.

The Surinam toad, now known as *Pipa pipa*, shown here in J. G. Wood's *Illustrated Natural History: Reptiles, Fishes, Molluscs* (1863).

treats its offspring in this manner. After the eggs are fertilized, the *D. pumilio* male tends the clutch on land, periodically urinating on them to keep them moist. When they have hatched, the female carries the tadpoles one by one to pockets of water in the forest plants, laying unfertilized eggs for them to eat. Up to six tadpoles per brood can be successfully raised to maturity in this way by a diligent pair of parents.

Tadpoles grow and develop gradually, but the final stage of metamorphosis to young frog is astonishingly quick and total, as little as 24 hours. The totality and co-ordination of the change is necessary to prevent the dangerous situation of the tadpole-frog being stranded in between forms, only half-adapted to its environment and helpless to the forces of natural selection. The filtering, scraping mouthparts must be transformed into predatory jaws, and the long, spiral gut necessary to digest algae gives

An early from-life
illustration of
a frog: Jan Ven
Kessel the Elder
(1626–79), *Dead
Tree Frog.*

way to a predator's short digestive tract. The skin thickens and
develops glands to keep the frog moist on land. Lungs are
present from early in the tadpole's life, but the pouch that previously contained the jaws must make way for the front legs.
Nerves and senses all undergo dramatic change; the eyes
develop massively to detect moving prey, and eyelids form to
protect the eyes on land. Only the tail remains for a while as a
sign of the frog's former life, physiologically unimportant com-

pared to other changes and eventually reabsorbed by the body. Metamorphosis is a remarkable feat, as yet only partially understood by scientists.

It is no wonder that philosophers, natural historians and scientists have long been intrigued by batrachians.[7] The study of frogs in the seventeenth and eighteenth centuries can be classed as natural history; comparative anatomy – a major component of evolutionary study – informed frog research in the late eighteenth and nineteenth centuries. Frogs went on to become subjects for physiologists and developmental biologists in the nineteenth and twentieth centuries respectively, and today the majority of herpetological publications concern anuran ecology.

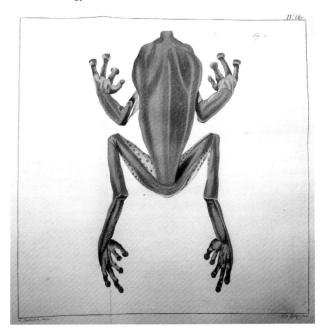

An unidentified blue and yellow frog from an early herpetological work: Joannes Albertus Schlosser, *De Lacerta Amboinensi* (1768).

Even within science, the frog is a creature of mythological dimensions. The frog on the scientist's bench is not a neutral tool of investigation, but comes sticky with culture: with the qualities and myths that are attributed to it. Such connotations started out in the early modern period as co-extensive with the myths of general knowledge, but as time went on science evolved a mythology of its own for the frog. Thus, as the following chapters recount, the frog has been a scientific embodiment of theological humility; a bundle of nerves; a bag of hormones; and an exemplar of evolution's extraordinary force. In the laboratory, it has been a creature both of vivaciousness and death.

The psychoanalyst Ernest Jones noted that the items most significant in myth and the unconscious often come in ambivalent form, auguring at once opposite qualities and significances.[8] So it is with the frog. The frog, as we shall see, stands for fecundity and sterility; for laughter and loss; for fortune and hopelessness; and for enlightenment and devilry.

The frog slips continually from our grasp, moving between its twin realms and trailing our fantasies in its watery wake.

1 Just a Kiss

Who would not desire the frog's powers of total transformation? Who would not wish to metamorphose from the realm of frustration and subordination to another world altogether: from the murky pond to the clear, bright air?

Hindu philosophical teaching in the Upanishad scriptures is one of the most ancient textual sources to suggest that frogs have something to teach us about metamorphosis of the self. The Mandukya Upanishad, also known as 'the frog', describes attainment of the very highest state of transcendence and the mystic syllable 'aum'. Some of the Mandukya's many devotees explain its name in relation to anuran locomotion – jumping, not walking. This scripture, they say, teaches that spiritual transition from one state of consciousness to another can only be achieved as a complete leap, like a frog's. Other commentators have instead likened the stillness of the yogi to that of the frog, which at rest manifests its vitality only by the gentle, rhythmic movements of its throat. Either way, the frog is co-opted by the human meditator as an agent of metamorphosis.

Bufotenine may be a quicker route to enlightenment than meditation, but it too comes from frogs; it is the chemical responsible for making you high when you smoke a toad.[1] There was a flurry of interest in the drug during the 1990s, with users claiming that it gave a gentle hallucinogenic rush and law-makers

A. I. Rösel fecit et exc.

declaring its dangers. In the southwestern states of the US, users were apparently milking the glands of the Sonoran desert toad, *Bufo alvarius*, for their secretions and drying them on car windscreens prior to smoking them in a pipe. (Most of this information, however, came from a single, somewhat unreliable, source: a Californian arrested by narcotics agents together with his four toads, Hans, Franz, Peter and Brian.) Newspaper articles at the time reported that people were licking toads to get high, but this was apparently dangerous as well as inaccurate; besides bufotenine, the glands also contain toxic substances that can only be safely destroyed by smoking. In Queensland, Australia, the authorities responded to the menace by declaring bufotenine a controlled substance and banning the possession of toad slime.

As frogs move from water to earth, so they perhaps signal the human possibility of moving from earth to air: in short,

Illustration of tadpole metamorphosis from Roesel von Rosenhof's *Historia Naturalis Ranarum Nostratium* (1758).

The cane toad (*Bufo marinus*) has been suspected of being used for narcotic purposes in Queensland, Australia.

resurrection. The earliest Christians in Egypt used the frog as a symbol of resurrection, their icon referencing the local frog goddess Heket, who helped Osiris rise from the dead. The early modern naturalist Jan Swammerdam also offered a reflection on the similarity of frog and human transformation, albeit in more doleful vein:

A frog eyes up a *trompe l'oeil* fly for consumption in this study by Hans Hoffman, late 16th century, oil on parchment.

> The infant-man, who lived before in the water of the amnion, now breathes the vital air, which rushes into his lungs, and dilates and extends them. But . . . his appendage of misfortunes and trouble, like the tail of the frog, yet adheres for a long time to him, for he is full

Ed Hill, 'Ah, You Dear Toad, I Will Have a Kiss', 20th century, print.

AH ! YOU DEAR TOAD, . I WILL HAVE A KISS .

of misery, and is born in tears; and it is very long before he comes to maturity of understanding, and full growth of body.[2]

The remainder of this chapter discusses in more detail two important transformations mediated by the frog in philosophy and folklore: from lead to gold, and from brute to royalty. If we could but hitch a ride with the frog, we could master the transformative secrets of alchemy or the kiss that yields a prince.

For hundreds of years, metamorphosis was above all studied in the guise of alchemy. Practitioners of the secret art sought the elixir that would turn base metal into gold and bring health and long life to its discoverer. Frogs, the premier animals of metamorphosis, were never far away, and the toad was a major element of alchemy's iconography, featuring on the title page of Elias Ashmole's influential *Theatrum Chemicum Britannicum* (1652). 'The Vision', a poem attributed to the revered Yorkshire alchemist George Ripley (1415–1490), similarly emphasized the batrachian element of alchemy in late medieval and early modern Europe. The poem begins:

A Toade full rudde I saw did drinke the juce of grapes so fast,
Till over charged with the broth, his bowells all to brast [burst].

The historian Jennifer Rampling demonstrates that Samuel Norton, who first discovered and translated the poem from Latin in 1573, glossed it as a fairly straightforward chemical recipe.[3] According to Norton, the ruddy toad stood for red lead, which, placed in strong wine vinegar, would absorb the liquid until it became reduced to prime matter. This *prima materia* was the fundamental, malleable stuff of creation, worked upon and perfected by alchemists just as Christ had perfected the human soul. The toad, turning into the *prima materia*, was the very origin of the alchemical process of metamorphosis.

Many alchemists shared Ripley's (or Norton's) association of the toad with the first stage of the alchemical process. One reason for the association was the appearance of the chemistry. Seething and digesting in the flask, the matter appeared black; and black, in terms of animal symbolism, was a toad. The alchemical toad's connection with putrefaction, sin (especially female) and blackness all indicated the fallen state of matter that must be perfected or saved by the alchemist.

During the late sixteenth century, Ripley's poetic writings on alchemy gave rise to around twenty illustrated scrolls. The scrolls, in which Ripley himself had no involvement, were substantial pieces, up to six metres long, expensive and precious; one was commissioned by the well-known polymath and occultist John Dee. The Ripley scrolls are all slightly different,

This detail from a Ripley Scroll (late 16th century) shows a toad in the centre of the alchemical alembic, and also at the top right of its smaller, contained roundels.

complex in their iconology, and comprise references to multiple sources. One common feature, however, is that toads appear frequently and prominently.

On a typical Ripley scroll the first depiction of the black toad comes at the top, contained within a hermetic vessel apparently held by Hermes Trismegestus himself, the mythical father of alchemy. Beneath this toad, within the vessel, are eight roundels linked to a central circle, each showing alchemists producing homunculi (miniature humanoids) in their vessels. The roundel in the one o'clock position, labelled *prima materia*, contains an Adam and Eve-like pair of figures, related to the Sun and

Moon; a very small toad can just be made out on the belly of the female Luna.

The generation of *prima materia* is retold lower down the manuscript, where a woman (labelled 'spiritus') holds onto a male child ('anima') who is almost falling from her. What is most striking about this woman is the green and tail-like thing emerging from between her buttocks. Scholars of the scroll have described this as a dragon's tail and it certainly does resemble the tail of the dragon further down the scroll. The image likely refers in part to the legend of Melusine, the woman whose lower half sometimes turned into a snake's, and who eventually transformed completely into a dragon. Although Rampling is sceptical that the similarity was intended,[4] the dragon's tail also looks strikingly like a ribbon of toadspawn being laid. Given the medieval slippage between serpents and batrachians, the connection would not seem impossible; indeed, the webbed feet of the woman might suggest it. A second verse on the scroll (also ascribed to Ripley) likewise suggests that the outcome of the mystical alchemical union, via a serpent form, is a toad:

> Then Earth on Fire shalbe put,
> And Water with Air shalbe knit,
> Thus ye shall go to Putrefaccion,
> And bring the Serpent to reduction.
> First he shalbe Black as any Crow,
> And downe in his Den shall lye full lowe:
> Iswel'd as a Toade that lyeth on ground . . .

Further still down the scroll, there is a dragon spitting out a toad (although in some other scrolls it looks more as though the toad is being swallowed). This toad is labelled with the caption 'the tayming venome', which associates the toad not just with the first stage, but also with the whole narrative trajectory of 'The Vision'. Although Ripley's poem is in part a practical recipe, there is also a strong Eucharistic tinge to it, focused by the toad. Upon receiving wine, the toad's sin-like poison causes him grief and pain, and is then purged from his body. After this, the toad turns black and dies in his cave and, akin to the phenomenon of resurrection, goes through a series of colour changes as part of the alchemical process. Ripley claims to extract a venom at the end of this procedure which, like God's judgement, can either kill or save depending on circumstances.

This secret treasure, contained in the toad and extracted by the magus, bore considerable resemblance to a trope of general folklore: the precious stone that was thought to be concealed within the heads of old toads. Variously described as a jewel or a panacea, the stone is mentioned by Shakespeare in *As You Like It*:

> Sweet are the uses of adversity;
> Which like the toad, ugly and venomous,
> Wears yet a precious jewel in his head.

Edward Fenton's *Secrete Wonders of Nature* (1569) was among many sources to agree that 'there is founde in the *heades* of old and great *toades*, a *stone* which they call Borax or Stelon . . . of power to repulse poysons'. Intriguingly, Chinese mythology includes a similar fable; the three-legged toad of the holy man Liu Hai produced a pearl in the night which, if ingested, would turn a man into a saint. The power of the toad stone was remarkably like the power of the philosopher's stone, though both, alas, were sadly elusive.

Just as the toadish *prima materia* contained a nugget of perfection, so alchemists figured part of their process as an allegory

The Grimms' Frog King story is much celebrated, including on this 1966 German Bundespost stamp.

in which the King's son went down into the sea, but retained a spark within him and was restored to life. 'Be turned unto me with all your heart and do not cast me aside because I am black and swarthy . . . and the waters have covered my face', begins one such parable, aligning the King's son with both the colour and the aqueous setting of the toad. Another account promises: 'Whosoever will free me from the waters and lead me to dry land, him will I prosper with everlasting riches.'[5] Such parables are tantalizingly close to tales of 'The Frog King'.

No one knows the age or provenance of the frog king tale before it was collected and written down by the Brothers Grimm. Sometimes a king, sometimes a prince, the batrachian of their story is now a staple of childhood fiction and popular culture. Traditionally, it is the very first of the tales in the Grimms' collection. One might not think that the story requires repeating, but its plot, as it first appeared to English-speaking audiences in 1823, may not be quite as is commonly remembered. A young princess drops her golden ball into a deep well, from which a frog promises to retrieve it on condition that she grants him favours – to let him live with her, to eat from her plate – and culminating with the right to sleep in her bed. Thinking that he will not be able to leave the well to claim his reward, she assents, only to have him turn up in the middle of dinner and remind her of her promise. The girl's father, the King, urges her to keep her word. Thus she goes through the list of actions, and is relieved to find the frog gone in the morning. The same thing happens the second night, and the third, and on the third

Arthur Rackham, illustration to the Brothers Grimm's 'Frog Prince', 1909.

morning she awakes to find a handsome prince at the foot of her bed, who reveals that he had been enchanted by a spiteful fairy, but that her actions have now undone the spell. And off they go to live happily ever after.

One immediately notices a striking fact: contrary to popular belief, the princess does not kiss the frog. In the initially unpublished transcription of 1810, there is another variant. The princess gingerly carries the frog up to her room on the first and only night of his visitation, and puts him in the corner of her room. When he insists on being put in her bed, she finally picks him up and flings him against the wall in disgust; when he falls down, he has made his transformation to handsome prince. It's

An early 20th-century German postcard illustrating a scene from 'The Frog King'.

The Frog King is an international fable, commemorated in its gender-inverted Russian form as the Tsarevna Frog, or Frog Princess.

a long way from a kiss. In the first published version of the tale (1812), the princess's violent action is removed by the Grimms, and replaced with the three-night visitation better known in English; however, later published versions in German and English reverted to the frog being flung against the wall.

It would be futile to seek for a truly original version of the tale. The Brothers Grimm collected two similar tales which were conflated by the first English translator, and numerous variants have since been gathered from around the world. Most feature not a princess but an ordinary girl from a poor family; a Breton version has, instead of a girl, a poor lad who is importuned by a female frog. In many versions, the girl goes to get not a golden ball but a drink from the well; often, she has two sisters who reject the water that has been made murky by the frog. Several accounts tell how the girl has been sent to collect water in a sieve from the 'well of the world's end'; the frog's demands come in return for giving her the handy hint that she should first line the sieve with moss. In tales from Scotland and the north of England, the frog begs to be put out of his misery if he cannot share the girl's bed, and it is decapitation that breaks the spell.[6]

One problem with all these stories is that they were gathered after the Brothers Grimm had published theirs. Indeed, the Grimms' book must have been in large part what inspired folklorists to collect them. Surely the writers, and perhaps even the tellers, had their tales inflected by the Grimms'. Inspired by the story, they were on the look-out for frogs; they may have been more inclined to hear the frog elements in other folklore, and to bend frog tales to the plot they had already read.

A Sri Lankan story, gathered in 1910, is nevertheless quite different from The Frog King, and does not suit modern European plot expectations at all. A widow bears a frog for a son, and this frog goes off to retrieve the jewelled golden cock from a local ogress, for which feat the King has promised half his kingdom. Setting out on his quest, the frog turns into a handsome man, and armed with magic charms from three other nearby kings, he gets the cock and defeats both the ogress and her daughter. Returning home, he turns back into a frog and the jewelled cock disappears. Understandably disappointed at this turn of events – everything seemed to be going so well! – he expires from grief.[7]

A Korean tale follows the European pattern more closely; an elderly couple adopt a giant frog who brings them great wealth; he demands to be married to a powerful neighbour's beautiful daughter, which feat at last they pull off, thanks in part to the tradition of covering a bride's eyes until the wedding night. At this point, the bride takes a knife to the frog, ostensibly at his own request but not without a certain willingness too. She thereby releases a silk-clad prince, son of the King of the Stars.[8] In a lengthy Chinese story, there is a nice twist on the Grimms' tale: the frog prince finally tricks the Emperor – who would not keep his promise to let his daughter marry him – into taking on his frog skin. The former frog lives on as a handsome man, now Emperor in his father-in-law's place.[9]

Despite the Grimms' claims to write things down just as they had been told them, 'The Frog King' underwent ideological changes and expansion in their successive revisions over several decades. Since then, the story has continued to go through all sorts of fashions and phases in its interpretation. Jack Zipes writes confidently that the tale 'underline[s] morals in keeping with the Protestant ethic and a patriarchal notion of sex roles'.[10] 'The male is [their] reward', Zipes comments of the Grimms' rare heroines, highlighting how the princess settles down to a life of domesticity under male governance. Similarly, the folklorist Lutz Röhrich points out how later Grimm versions make more of the girl's father's authority in forcing her to accede to the frog's demands. Feminists have understandably taken issue with this, just as they have with the supposed happy ending of the tale. Who wants to give up playing with a golden ball and become a wifely possession of a king, however handsome? One jokey re-take on the story thus culminates instead with the girl, proudly single, enjoying sautéed frogs' legs. Although feminist critiques of the patriarchal father are in one sense valid, patriarchy does not appear to be central to early nineteenth-century versions of the tale, because it is usually a mother or widow who insists on the girl's acquiescence, out of a sense of honour in sticking to one's word. Women, of course, reinforce patriarchy just as much as men, but in this nineteenth-century tale at least the frog's 'frogness' trumped its masculinity; it was not to be obeyed on the strength of the latter quality.

Just as the king becomes more insistent in some versions of the tale, so does the princess become correspondingly more resistant. Most critics of recent years are agreed on the sexual element of the tale that is indicated by this resistance: that it portrays 'crises related to thoughts of marrying or the wedding night'.[11] The princess is a young woman on the verge of sexual maturity and marriage, and the frog's requests escalate in intimacy to the unmistakeable level of sharing her bed. In fact, the pre-publication version of the Grimms' tale had *only* the explicitly sexual request to sleep with her; the brothers appear to have inserted the other two to tone things down. (The psychoanalyst Bruno Bettelheim cites a still earlier version in which the girl must kiss the frog while it lies by her side in bed, and then sleeps with him for three whole weeks before his transformation.) Having taken out the violence in the first published version – replacing the wall-throwing with three nights of bed-sharing – the brothers appeared to have thought better of the latter and reverted to the violence as morally preferable to sex.

These changes reflect an omnipresent anxiety about the nature of 'The Frog Prince'; it has frequently been described as an erotic tale that is not really meant for children at all. The psychoanalyst Ernest Jones offered the most famous and probably the original such interpretation in 1928:

> [T]he frog is in the unconscious a constant symbol of the male organ when viewed with disgust. So . . . the story represents the maiden's gradual overcoming of her aversion to intimacy with this part of the body.[12]

The critic Karen Rowe goes one stage further, explaining animal bridegrooms as a manifestation of the Electra complex (an alternative version of Freud's Oedipus, in which the girl desires her father). According to Rowe, the animal plays a substitute's role within the tale, onto which the girl's unspeakable love may be safely displaced.[13] If Ernest Jones had written more than a single paragraph on the story, he might perhaps have gone in the same direction as Rowe. Jones emphasizes elsewhere that hollow items in stories are images of the vagina or womb, but does not dwell on the fact – surprisingly, considering his interpretative framework – that the frog is *already* in the well at the beginning of the tale. Whose is the well? Could it be the mother's? Could discovery of the parents' sexual intimacy, and jealousy of it disguised as horror, be the prompt that sets the girl on her quest? If only Jones had spent more time on the story.

Bruno Bettelheim (building on the work of Joseph Campbell and Carl Jung) was comfortable both with the sexual nature of the tale and its childish audience.[14] To him, fairy tales in general, and tales of animal bridegrooms in particular, were a healthy way of helping children work through issues that could not and should not be presented to them overtly. Repression was less pathological for Bettelheim than for Freud: it was simply a normal life-stage that needed to be out-grown. Fairy tales were, for him, a means for the child to do this out-growing: a way to learn about the stages of selfhood, identity, maturity before they were encountered.

Bettelheim is one of very few critics (apart from Jones and his confident aside) who engages the question of why a frog in particular works so well as a bestial groom. For one thing, the transformative nature of the frog's life cycle echoes his child-to-adult treatment of fairy tales. More importantly, however, Bettelheim concludes that the frog is distinguished as an animal that inspires disgust but not genuine fear – that is, fear of the truly life-threatening. As the Grimms wrote: 'She was afraid of the cold frog, which she did not like to touch, and which was now to sleep in her pretty, clean little bed.' A Bantu fable cited by Bettelheim has a girl kiss a crocodile to effect his transformation – an entirely more challenging proposition. Earlier versions of 'The Frog King', in which the creature is a snake or a dragon, have indeed slipped from the collective memory, suggesting that these more fearsome creatures no longer suit our post-medieval concerns about sexuality. (Such frightening creatures were generally princesses in disguise rather than princes, in keeping with the medieval identification of sexual sin with womankind.)[15] Focusing the signified of batrachian disgust still more specifically, Bettelheim notes the phallic propensity of the frog to 'puff up'.

In composing the song 'Kiss That Frog' (1993), Peter Gabriel seems to have read Bettelheim, or else has pulled the erotic themes of the frog from the communal ether. As far I know, he is the only person to put together the kissing of popular myth with the phallic frog of academic criticism, working them in the form of a sexually knowing song that is at once funny and seductive. 'He's all puffed up . . . kiss it better . . .'. Contributors to an online discussion board on the topic (songfacts.com) are mostly persuaded that the song is at least partly about oral sex, except for one poster from Massachusetts who insists against all interpretative odds: 'After Listening to it thouroly I Beleave its About Princess Dianna and Prince Charles and how she was so beautiful and he Ugly and mean to her [sic]'.

Bettelheim's pedagogical role for 'The Frog King' is by no means unique. Educators and agitators of all sorts have re-written and re-interpreted the story to suit their ends. One does not fully appreciate the Grimms' lightness of touch until one reads the well-meaning efforts of many of these imitators. Geoff

Dench, for example, uses the story to interrogate the 'problem of men' in post-feminist society, noting the 'social peripherality of the frog's location' (by which he means the woods). 'Women want men to be responsible like themselves', he concludes: to move away from the marginal, superficial world of 'frog culture' and become real princes.[16] Barbara G. Walker's version in *Feminist Fairy Tales* (1996) has a female frog protagonist who kisses a male, becomes human, and then spends her happy-ever-after life on her own. Female frogs, Walker notes solemnly in her introduction, make a good role model for feminists as they are larger than their males. My personal favourite, however, is J. F. Konrad's 1981 tale 'Der Lustfrosch' (the lecherous frog). At first concerned only with seduction, the frog sees the disgust and suffering that he thereby causes his inamorata and ceases in his efforts. Recognizing his newfound humanity, the princess begins to treat him with compassion. It's not so much the tale as its raison d'être which is enjoyable for its earnestness. Konrad explains:

> The revision has been conceived with a view toward adolescents and is intended to help in connection with other media and texts to free sex and eros from egotism, exploitation, and boasting, and also from inhibition, besmirching and smut and so enable them to form a partnership that lives from consideration and fulfilment.[17]

Despite applauding Konrad's aim, one cannot help but find oneself wishing for a little exploitation after all; perhaps even – whisper it – smut.

The oeuvre of the Disney studio is emphatically not the place to go looking for smut. Its animation *The Princess and the Frog* (2009) is a typically clean-cut rendering of mythology, in this case of the Grimms' tale. It is also, as the title suggests, an instantiation of a trend that has been going on for some time, namely a shift in interest from the frog prince to the princess – or rather the girl, as she starts out. In a limited sense therefore the film echoes Walker's tale, entitled 'The Frog Princess', although the female focus of the Disney version is some way from women's liberation as it is recognized by serious feminists.

Disney's film blends the plot from the Brothers Grimm tale with a then-recently published novel for young adults entitled, like Walker's tale, *The Frog Princess* (E. D. Baker, 2002). In this version, a girl kisses a frog in the hopes of becoming a princess but instead, and unhappily, finds herself transformed into a frog. The film too was originally to be known as *The Frog Princess*; Disney's pre-release market research, however, suggested that the proposed title was considered by some to be a slur against French people and it was changed accordingly.

The movie was made at a time when Disney's fortunes were failing. The computer-generated animations of Pixar and Dream-Works were all the rage, while Disney had suffered a series of flops with its recent traditional animations. In 2004, Disney closed its 2D studios, but failed to find great success with its first 3D animation (*Chicken Little*, 2005) either. Meanwhile, however, Disney princess merchandise – launched without much market research in 2001 – had achieved astonishing commercial success. Little girls apparently couldn't get enough of the princessy theme. The annual value of sales based on the established characters of Cinderella et al. was estimated at around $3bn in 2006 ($4bn by 2010); anyone with half a business brain could see the chance for one more sure-fire, big hit. So, when Disney bought Pixar in 2006, they re-opened the traditional animation studio. There was one big princess story still to go.

The *Princess and the Frog* very gently shakes up the recipe for Disney fairy stories, most obviously by having the studio's

Still from Lotte Reiniger's silhouette animation *The Frog Prince* (1954).

first-ever black princess character, and also slightly rewriting the Grimms' tale. Turned into a frog by a voodoo spell, Prince Naveen is on the look-out for a princess – he knows the kissing deal – and mistakes the waitress Tiana, in a borrowed costume, for being what he needs. On being kissed, however, she too is transformed into a frog and together the pair escape to the Louisiana swamp where the voodoo queen Mama Odie lives; eventually, and despite many complications, Odie succeeds in guiding them to break the spell.

Tiana is more independent-minded than her princess predecessors. Her idea of a happy ever after – which of course she achieves – is to run her own business. Anika Noni Rose, the actor who voiced Tiana, stated: 'She's a strong woman who doesn't need anyone to do things for her . . . She wants to do things for herself.' Nevertheless, love and marriage are an essential part of the resolution. Naveen is transformed through his interactions with Tiana, becoming less selfish and vain until he metamorphoses into the perfect groom. (Just like real-life elite European-American marriages of the early twentieth-century era in which the tale is set, the transaction buys him money and her a pedigree.)

The sense that the frog is simply waiting to be exploited for his royal connections has its roots in the beautiful silhouette animation of the tale made by Lotte Reiniger in 1954. This widely disseminated film sets in place what is now a key feature of batrachian iconology, the crown on the frog. This headgear is a major clue for Tiana (or rather the film's viewers – somehow she seems to miss it) that this is not your average sort of frog. The coronet on Reiniger's frog is identical to the princess's, foretelling their ultimate compatibility. Indeed, Reiniger's tale, like its twenty-first-century successors, is about marriage from the outset. The girl's father, the King, says the golden ball will bring royal marriage to its owner and throws it to his three daughters to see which one can catch it.

The frog is ruefully celebrated as a feature of the contemporary dating game, as this image from a dating advice website shows.

The title-shift from the Grimms' story to the movie (from the frog's identity to the girl's) thus changes to a focus on the female narrative – the girl's ambition and desire to secure a happy ending for herself. Like the heroine of Baker's story, Tiana aims, in kissing her frog, not at marrying a prince but rather *at becoming a princess*. Maybe the writer on the Peter Gabriel site was right: the aspirational 'Tiana' is not so far from 'Diana', after all.

How did we get from decapitation to a kiss? Today, in the West, sex is no longer so feared and dreaded that a symbolic act as severe as decapitation is required for us to capitulate to our desires. In today's account of the Grimms' tale, the aim is only secondarily to find love. Primarily it is about becoming a princess – an act of self-realization whose final stage is, thanks to the frog, an erasure of the processes that have earned 'success' and

Still from the Disney film *The Princess and the Frog* (dir. John Musker and Ron Clements, 2009).

a validation of that success (fame, celebrity, being worth it) as if it had been assumed by right, like a royal inheritance. The frog groom is no longer significant in himself, but only insofar as he enables the girl's metamorphosis. The chief purpose of the fairy tale is, as the UK wedding business of the same name states, to be 'princess for a day'.

2 Warts and All

Carl Linnaeus' view of the Amphibia was not, by today's standards, what you would call a model of objectivity. In his authoritative edition of the *Systema Naturae* (1758), he wrote:

> These foul and loathsome animals are distinguished by a heart with a single ventricle and a single auricle, doubtful lungs and a double penis. Most amphibia are abhorrent because of their cold body, pale colour, cartilaginous skeleton, filthy skin, fierce aspect, calculating eye, offensive smell, harsh voice, squalid habitation, and terrible venom; and so their Creator has not exerted his powers [to create] many of them.[1]

Most of these characteristics can be found in traditional representations of frogs. Their imperfect physiology, epitomized by their need to metamorphose, made them theologically dubious from the Middle Ages and into the early modern period. The mystifying double penis – for of course frogs have none, let alone two – can probably be explained by the lumping together of amphibians and reptiles in Linnaeus' day; the latter do indeed possess this remarkable anatomical feature. The routine grouping of amphibians and reptiles put frogs in the same group as that satanic creature, the snake. Frogs' and toads'

Frogs have been popularly associated with naughty boys, although here the teacher appears to turn the tables.

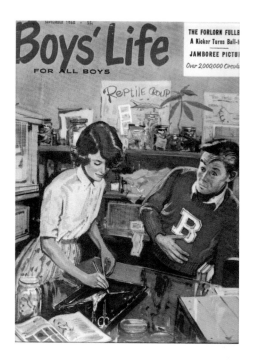

association with damp places, and their supposed venomousness, have also long counted against them. To Linnaeus' list of reasons for abhorrence we might also add the unpredictable nature of batrachians' movement, a quality that frogs share with the suddenly scuttling spider. It's the unexpected 'boing' of a frog, guaranteed to raise a shriek, that makes them such a satisfying surprise resident of the teacher's desk. The horizontal slit-form of the pupil visible in some frogs and toads is also for some reason disconcerting, a characteristic shared with that other demonic creature, the goat. And, lastly, the squatting posture of the frog perhaps reminds us humans of our own in defecation.

Of frogs and toads, the latter definitely have the worse press. Milton had Satan himself 'squat like a Toad, close at the eare of Eve' in *Paradise Lost*. The natural philosopher Lazzaro Spallanzani apologized for writing about toads in his *Dissertations*; although the batrachian was not devilish, nevertheless '[n]ice and fastidious persons may perhaps be disgusted at the frequent mention of an animal so loathsome . . . *disagreeable, nauseous* &c.'.[2] The toad's well-known (and entirely spurious) propensity to cause warts apparently requires refutation to this day in every factual account of the animals aimed at a general audience.

Toads have been almost universally considered to be venomous. The very word 'toady', a sycophant, refers to this property. In the early modern period, a toady was the sidekick of a charlatan, employed to eat (or pretend to eat) toads, thus enabling his master to exhibit his skill in expelling poison. Edward

Bufo cornutus (now reclassified as *Ceratophrys cornuta*), complete with horns and leering mouth, appeared to confirm the toad's devilish reputation. From François Marie Daudin's *Histoire Naturelle des Rainettes, des Grenouilles et des Crapauds* (1803).

Topsell, in his *History of Serpents*, gave considerable attention to the venom of frogs and toads. Among the effects of frog poisoning were a swelling-up of the body and pallidness; bad breath and difficulty in breathing; an 'involuntary profusion of seed'; and general dullness and restlessness. Even toad-spit on the scalp, noted Topsell, was enough to cause baldness. For Boccaccio, the breath was enough to cause mischief. In the *Decameron* a couple dies after rubbing their gums with sage leaves; a toad is later found among the roots of the plant, infecting it with its poisonous exhalations. Truly, the venom of the toad was something to be feared, although sometimes good fortune might save one from apparently certain toad-related death. In a 'noted story' of 1617, a country-dweller awoke from a nap to find that a 'Toad [had] fixed himself upon the mouth & outside of [his] lips'. So firmly was the toad clamped on that violence was needed to remove it; yet this could not be attempted lest the toad was thereby induced to spit his poison 'which he uses as his offensive & defensive weapon'. Fortunately, a nearby spider, being the natural enemy of the toad, provided the solution. Upon being stung twice by this beast, the toad 'swelled & fell dead'.[3]

The very potency of frog venom also made it an exceptionally powerful medicine, and Topsell gave numerous recipes for its use. Here he was largely inspired by Pliny the Elder, whose 32nd book of the *Natural History* was positively stuffed with frog remedies. Frogs' blood, fat, flesh, eyes, heart, liver, gall, entrails, legs and sperm were all efficacious. They could be used as powders, distillations, broth and infusions; they were good for leprosy, scabs, poisoning, dropsie, coughs, gout and much more. Buried in the garden (as for example in Thomas Hyll's 1572 *Arte of Gardeninge*), a toad would drive away pests.

The noted early nineteenth-century savant Georges Cuvier announced that toads in fact contained no venom, but in 1851 and 1852, two French philosophers were reported still to be attempting to sort fact from fiction, experimenting with poison extracted from the skin of toads. They succeeded in partially paralysing a 'little African tortoise' and in killing a goldfinch. The correspondent reporting their experiments to *The Zoologist* noted that Messieurs Gratiolet and Cloez were at this time 'occupied in collecting a large amount of toad-venom', but ominously enough no information was forthcoming on their intended use for this chemical weaponry.[4]

The notion of the unpalatable nature of frogs goes back a long way. In Levitical law, the frog was proclaimed by implication to be unclean. 'These shall ye eat of all that are in the waters: whatsoever hath fins and scales in the waters, in the seas, and in the rivers, them shall ye eat . . . Whatsoever hath no fins nor scales in the waters, that shall be an abomination unto you' (Leviticus 11:9–12). However, the chief damage to the frog's reputation occurred thanks to Moses and his repeated attempts to encourage Pharaoh in the matter of Israelite emigration (Exodus 8:2–4):

And if thou refuse to let them go [Moses warns Pharaoh],
behold, I will smite all thy borders with frogs:
And the river shall bring forth frogs abundantly, which
shall go up and come into thine house, and into thy
bedchamber, and upon thy bed, and into the house of
thy servants, and upon thy people, and into thine
ovens, and into thy kneadingtroughs:
And the frogs shall come up both on thee, and upon thy
people, and upon all thy servants.

And so it proves to be. The thought of kneading down on bread and squashing frogs instead, or finding them in bed and in the oven, is really rather unpleasant. Pharaoh's magicians

Alluding to the Mosaic plague, frogs fall from the sky in this poster for the film *Magnolia* (dir. Paul Thomas Anderson, 1999).

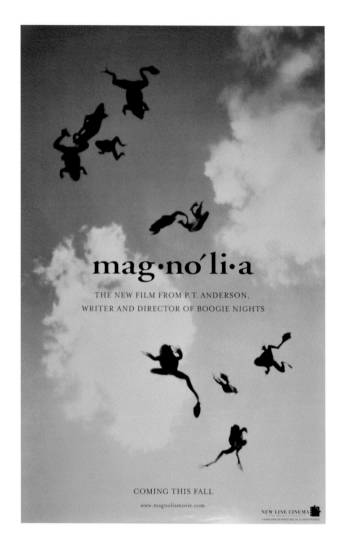

TAB. CXXV

EXODI Cap VIII. v 2-14.
Ranarum Forma et Metamorphosis

II Buch Mosis Cap VIII. v. 2-14.
Frosch-gestalt und Verwandlung

Johannes Jacob Scheuchzer, *Exodus: The Plague of Frogs*, from *Physica Sacra*, engraving, 1731–5.

are able to duplicate Moses' trick, but alas cannot perform the altogether more useful feat of making them disappear. When Moses does so instead, things are little better: the people 'gathered them together upon heaps: and the land stank' (8:14).

The biblical plague has provoked numerous later reports of frogs falling as precipitation. The phenomenon is one of those widely known 'facts' that is actually rather hard to find in well-evidenced form, beyond meteorologists agreeing that in

principle a small tornado might pick up and then dump small creatures such as frogs. The film *Magnolia* (1999) ends with a downpour of frogs, a surprising conclusion to an otherwise realistic film. Many viewers claim to find references to the biblical story hidden throughout the movie. Elsewhere, the phenomenon is purely proverbial; in Polish and Romanian, it is not cats and dogs, but rather frogs that fall from the sky during heavy rain.

Tainted by the Torah with pagan magic, frogs went on to appear in the book of Revelation (16:12–14) as evil spirits:

> And the sixth angel poured out his vial upon the great river Euphrates; and the water thereof was dried up, that the way of the kings of the east might be prepared. And I saw three unclean spirits like frogs come out of

the mouth of the dragon, and out of the mouth of the beast, and out of the mouth of the false prophet. For they are the spirits of devils, working miracles . . .

The power of frogs (and toads, and newts) to work miracles has been widely believed ever since such ancient writings, at least in European mythology. Perhaps it is also their metamorphic nature that makes them such potent agents of transformation. Shakespeare's witches knew well the devilish virtues of frogs and toads:

First Witch: Round about the cauldron go;
In the poison'd entrails throw.
Toad, that under cold stone
Days and nights has thirty one
Swelter'd venom sleeping got,
Boil thou first i' the charmed pot.

Second Witch: . . . Eye of newt and toe of frog,
Wool of bat and tongue of dog,

All: . . . Double, double toil and trouble;
Fire burn, and cauldron bubble.

In *Faust*, too, Mephistopheles includes frogs and toads in his recipe to help a blonde with her troublesome freckles. Such potions were apparently not just in use in fiction. The historian Deborah Willis tells how, on Lammas Eve 1590, a group of 40 witches set out to kill the King with a poison concocted from 'toad, adderskin and other vile materials'.[5] In 1608, Edward Topsell noted that witches preferred toad venom as the means by which to poison their husbands.

Frogs and toads were not just the ingredients in satanic brews; they were also the active assistants of witches, one form of the demonic sidekicks known as familiars. Mephistopheles describes how they do his bidding; he is 'The master of the rats and mice/ Of flies and frogs, of bugs and lice'. The anthropologist Margaret Murray noted that witches generally kept their frog and toad familiars in a pot or box and fed them on magically significant foods. Fifteenth-century witch-hunters recounted a tale of a witch who placed the Eucharistic bread in a pot with her toad, while Murray highlighted witches' frequent use of breast milk to nurture their batrachians. The demonic nature of this phenomenon forced Michael Maier to explain in his alchemical text *Atalanta Fugiens* (1617) that his emblem of a woman suckling a toad was not to be taken literally. 'It is indeed a thing ominous for a Toad to be born of Woman', he clarified, and you can't really argue with that. Beliefs about batrachian familiars were not just in the currency of fable; in 1645, for example, a witch found to have an imp in the form of a frog was hanged in Cambridge.[6]

It was in the context and period of such hangings that the eminent English physician William Harvey (1578–1657) is commonly supposed to have disproved the existence of demonic toads. According to the story, at some time in the 1630s Harvey disguised himself as a wizard and talked his way into a witch's dwelling, where he asked to see her toad familiar. He then sent her off to buy some ale, during which time he dissected the toad. Upon opening its belly, he found that it had real milk inside, and concluded that this was no magical beast but merely, in the splendid phrase of the tale's author, 'an arrant naturall toad'.

A woman gives birth to a toad before her child, from Jacob van Maerlant's *Der Naturen Bloeme* (c. 1350).

The witch proved sadly recalcitrant when it came to accepting this experimental disproof of her powers. Far from capitulating to Harvey's demonstration, she 'threw downe the pitcher of ale, [and] flew like a tigris at his face'. Harvey was then forced to try the decidedly non-scientific methods of bribery and finally blackmail to get her to accept his conclusions, revealing that he was the King's physician and threatening to have her prosecuted and hanged.

As historian Cathy Gere explains, the witch was not the only one to doubt Harvey's proof. The anecdote, she argues, is as problematic as such other scientific myths as Newton and the apple.[7] James Long, who wrote down the events in 1686 on the basis of conversations with Harvey, himself judged that this was a 'weake experiment'. Gere highlights how Long caricatures the tenuousness of Harvey's argument: that 'the toad . . . had really eaten milk and not in appearance only, [and that] therefore there are no witches'. Long's counter-argument ('Spirits have recourse to toades . . . at set times . . . but doe not exert them constantly') seems to boil down to the idea that the witch might have a natural toad (therefore anatomically normal) that was sometimes possessed by an exterior spirit. Conceivably Long's argument implied that the toad would appear internally normal even at the times that it was thus possessed: that there was no difference between its inside and outside in this respect. Gere's account shows that Harvey by no means established a definitively rational view of the frog. 'Scientific' and 'superstitious' views of batrachians continued to co-exist through the early modern period.

Edward Topsell's account of frogs (reprinted the year after Harvey's death) is a perfect illustration of Gere's argument. In it, Topsell is most concerned to distinguish 'natural' and 'magical' properties of the frog. The latter have no place in true learning;

he dismisses one instance with the robust judgement: 'this is as true as [that] a shoulder of Mutton worn in one's Hat healeth the tooth-ach'. Yet, to the modern reader, Topsell's examples of the natural properties of frogs are scarcely any different from their magical ones. Witches, for example, don't make spells with them; they just use their venom. Physicians, on the other hand, will find their healing frog broths work best if the patient doesn't know what he is drinking. Topsell's distinctions between nature and magic are not at root metaphysical but rather theological. Action at a distance, and through the hidden sympathies and powers of natural kinds, are all a part of his world.

Let us backtrack in time to discover why natural philosophy, or natural magic, made the toad a likely vehicle for malign spiritual influence. The answers lie in medieval theology, itself drawing on the work of the Ancient Greeks. Aristotle noted that some animals were generated spontaneously by putrefaction – as, for example, maggots and flies arise from a corpse. When these creatures then reproduced normally, he observed that they produced imperfect forms, meaning that they had to metamorphose to reach their final, adult form. Thomas Aquinas (1225–1274) gave the question of corruption and putrefaction a theological spin; the body's tendency to undergo this process was in contrast to the incorruptibility of the soul. (Plotinus [204/5–270] had in fact used the Greek term 'amphibian' to describe this duality, contrasting the rational and animal elements of human nature.) The Thomist theology of the corruptible body was encapsulated by Ecclesiasticus 10:11: 'For when a man is dead, he shall inherit creeping things, beasts and worms.' When one added the Aristotelian metamorphosis of the frog to its negative biblical connotations, it became a certain candidate for generation by putrefaction.

Frogs and toads also played a role in more general accounts of abominable birth and generation. English folklore in particular is rich with tales of toads incubating birds; one particular combination (toad and chicken) results in the monstrous basilisk.[8] Medieval tales of frogs and toads discovered sealed within stones or rock persisted well into the nineteenth century. Although nineteenth-century commentators attempted to give such accounts a non-magical explanation, the stories themselves were still regarded as utterly credible for the most part. Their origin and persistent appeal lay in their apparent evidence for the spontaneous generation of batrachians.

Malleus Maleficarum, the well-known 1486 treatise on witchcraft, synthesized Aristotelian and Thomist learning in order to tackle the question of whether witches could create animals (or turn people into animals).[9] Witches, its authors found, could indeed perform these feats, but only using Aristotle's imperfect animals – such as the frog (along with mice and serpents). Witches could essentially harness the process of putrefaction to produce these animals, as could (or so he claimed) the seventeenth-century Jesuit scholar Athanasius Kircher, using 'fertile dust'.

Transmutation – the changing of one creature into another – was dealt with by the *Malleus* in a similar manner. Magicians could counterfeit God's ability to transform the essence of matter, altering the superficial properties of humans into those of animals. Claiming the authority of Aquinas, the *Malleus* authors explained that frogs were a particularly suitable choice for the changing of humans; their externally scattered semen could easily be gathered and used by magicians to effect transmutation, to the same end result (the counterfeit creation of a frog) that would be produced by the semen through putrefaction. The authors of the *Malleus* noted that witches sometimes did not even create the superficial properties of a frog when they

Sigimondo Fanti, *Triompho di Fortuna*, 1526, engraving.

68

ROTA DELLA RANA

magicked a human, but merely their *appearance*. However, being only apparently changed into a frog was no less serious than being changed in reality since everyone – even the injured party – would truly and completely now perceive a frog in the victim's place. In such theological complexities we see the essence of Long's dispute with Harvey. There was no reason why a demonically derived toad should not be perceived as normal, even under the skin.

Edward Topsell was still bothered by the question of generation by putrefaction in the seventeenth century. His overarching programme in *The History of Serpents* was to show that all creatures gave 'testimony of God' by demonstrating that they were created by him. However, by the time he got to describing frogs, this conviction seems to have palled. He observed that their organs were 'corrupted', and gave a standard Aristotelian account of how 'some of them [were] engendered by carnal copulation, and [some] of the slime and rottennesse of the earth'. In other words, he was back to generation by putrefaction. Tales of women giving birth to frogs were particularly problematic for Topsell, for they introduced a perturbing blurring of the corrupt frog body and the God-resembling human body. He papered over the issue in one case-study by assuring the reader of the woman's good recovery; and in general he excused such cases by pointing out that they tended to befall Roman Catholics. The implication was that frog-birth was a result of their worshipping the whore of Babylon and her unclean, batrachian spirits.

Frogs born of putrefaction also took their place in medieval tomb decoration. During the fourteenth century, idealized images of the deceased began to be replaced by gruesome images of the dead and decaying body, the 'creeping things' of Ecclesiasticus.[10] These corpses covered by frogs and snakes

The deceased lovers of an unknown 15th-century artist show the use of frogs and toads in *memento mori*-type iconography.

became especially popular in Germany and Austria during the fifteenth and sixteenth centuries; a particularly good example remains in La Sarraz, Vaud (Switzerland). The wealthy de la Sarra family commissioned their tomb around the late fourteenth century and it includes a full-size, three-dimensional sculpture of a naked male corpse covered with snakes or worms; there is one frog on each eye, two on the mouth, and one on the genitals.

Commissioned by the rich, such iconology displayed appropriately humble confession of the sinful body prior to judgement. The creeping things that emerged by putrefaction from the body were like the sins that lurked within it. As Kathleen Cohen has noted, there were many examples of this trope at work in medieval German teaching. One thirteenth-century allegory told of a woman who would not confess to a particular sin; an angel appeared to her with a beautiful child, whose back revealed itself to be infested with toads and worms. The angel explained to the woman that this was the woman's condition while she remained unshriven. A similar image archetype, 'The Tempter' consisted of a young man, handsome from the front but writhing with frogs and snakes behind. A thirteenth-century monk from Heilsbronn dubbed the body 'Krotsack, Madensack' (sack of toads, sack of maggots), and another preacher of the same era called sins 'Kröten des Teufel' (toads of the devil).

Besides its connection to devilish putrefaction, the frog of the devil was largely to blame because of its posture, squatting on its victim like a demon. It was particularly associated with avarice. In the early seventeenth century, Edward Topsell described how toads would spend the winter clawing earth into their mouths to sustain them; their paws were constantly filled with earth, as though they were afraid they would run out, and in this they resembled the avaricious man who feared dying in

Avarice is portrayed as a frog in this print made by Jakob von der Heyden (1590–1645).

penury. Thus George Pencz, in his sixteenth-century engravings of sin, used the frog to symbolize avarice, punished by being placed in cauldrons of boiling oil.

For poet Philip Larkin, (1922–1985) the squatting toad was the curse of work. 'Why should I let the toad work/ Squat on my life?' he complained in 1954 in 'Toads'; 'Six days of the week it soils/ With its sickening poison'. However, Larkin found that the devil-may-care attitude necessary to scorn pensions and shoes – the things that work buys – was lacking in him. He identified this protestant ethic as a second toad, or 'something sufficiently toad-like/ [that] Squats in me, too'. 'Toads Revisited' (1962) reaches the same conclusion. Resigning himself to continued labours, Larkin invites his demon: 'Give me your arm, old toad;/ Help me down Cemetery Road.' In the summer of 2010, Larkin's home city of Hull celebrated his life with appropriate glum wit, commissioning a series of 40 giant, brightly coloured toad sculptures that were scattered through its streets. Suitably toad-like, many local politicians squatted on the project

Philip Larkin's 'toad, work' was commemorated in a witty and colourful series of outdoor toad sculptures in Hull in 2010. This one is decorated as the poet himself.

(named 'Plague of Toads'), complaining at its squandering of public money.

In his novel *Under The Frog* (1992), Tibor Fischer refers to the Hungarian expression that summarizes the unpleasant experience of being squatted on by a batrachian. In its full version, 'under the frog's arse at the bottom of the coal pit', it describes a situation that is as bad as it can possibly be. Although unpleasant characteristics of frogs – including their tendency to inhabit the marshy borders of Hades – go back to antiquity, it was in the Middle Ages that they were truly cemented as icons of ill. However, an important question remains: were the actual creatures regarded as evil, or were they simply used as a representation thereof? The historian Sophie Page writes that the real animals of the lived medieval experience were cognitively distinct from their existence as emblematic and symbolic creatures.[11] In real life, non-threatening animals at least were generally perceived as wholesome creations of God. Only in mythology and religious fable did they reflect or personify the devil. The reason for this separation of the real and the symbolic, she argues, was that theologians had been compelled to counter the Cathar heresy – which preached the inherent evil of the body, including the animal body – by asserting the goodness of beasts. However, crushing the Cathar heresy seems a long way from seventeenth-century England, and we have seen evidence to complicate Page's assessment. In 1608, Edward Topsell was still concerned with the putrid generation of frogs, and linked it to their treatment as primarily noxious animals. The story of William Harvey

One of the most horrific frogs ever must be the monstrous toad of *Pan's Labyrinth* (dir. Guillermo del Toro, 2006).

This affectionate 19th-century Japanese print of a toad reminds us that toads are not intrinsically uncongenial creatures as European tradition holds (School of Hokusai).

and the toad suggests that the possibility of physical evil was considered seriously enough for it to be worth telling in the late seventeenth century (even if his encounter didn't actually happen in reality). Hence, we wind up back where we started, with Linnaeus's surprising commentary on the animal. Much of his scientific representation of the 'foul and loathsome' frog remains with us to this very day.

3 Them, Us and Frogs

In 1970, when many Californian students were busy dropping acid, a young biologist named Richard Wassersug was persuading his postgraduate colleagues at Berkeley to eat tadpoles instead. It was all in the cause of science; his hypothesis was that highly visible species of tadpole must taste bad in order to put off predators, while those that are well-hidden do not need this additional defence. Duly following Wassersug's instructions to suck, bite, chew and rinse, the students gave taste-ratings for various species and substantiated his theory.[1] The arresting quality of the experiment gained Wassersug an Ig Nobel Prize, rewarding him for 'improbable research' that made people 'laugh and then think'. As Wassersug's award indicates, the eating of frogs is an attention-grabbing act, beset with cultural anxiety across many parts of the globe. This chapter explores how such anxiety is just a part – albeit a major one – of a bigger phenomenon: the use of frogs to make generalizations about nationality and ethnicity. Examples range from China to India, but most especially concern frogs in France and Australia.

Uneasiness about the consumption of frogs is closely associated with the difficulties that we have already seen in categorizing anurans; in anthropological terms, the categorization as edible or inedible, clean or unclean, is a fundamental one. We might expect creatures that are problematic and variable in

A pair of fresh frog's legs prepared for cooking.

their categorization – like frogs – to display the same properties in relation to their presumed edibility, and indeed this is borne out by observation. In southern China, for example, frogs are divided into three sorts: ha-ma, wa and toads, and different cultures in the region variously encourage, permit or revile the eating of each of these. In Sichuan during the Tang dynasty, ha-ma frogs were captured whilst copulating and popped on the dinner plate; they were also reared from tadpoles for consumption. Nearby outsiders objected to these customs as 'barbarian'. Wa frogs, on the other hand, were widely consumed across southern China.[2] Similarly, the 1891 census of Andhra Pradesh named the Kappala sub-group of the local Yanadi people as 'frog-eaters' and distinguished them from the 'non-frog-eater' sub-group. An inhabitant of the region reported that the Yanadis of the North Arcot district – the 'non-frog-eaters' – did not even permit the Kappala to touch their pots, so unclean was the latter's habit of batrachian consumption.[3]

The British and Americans are famously obsessed with the alleged passion of the French for consuming frogs' legs. The habit just does not seem right to Britons, even to many of those who otherwise consider themselves as adventurous eaters. The Scottish naturalist John Claudius Loudon (1783–1843), for example, suggested several foreign animals that might be cultivated for

The European edible frog. Although it is often given as the species *Rana esculenta*, it is actually a fertile hybrid of the pool frog (*Pelophylax lessonae*) and the marsh frog (*Pelophylax ridibundus*).

the pot on the estates of the gentry, but stopped short at the Edible Frog (*Rana esculenta*). Although it was a common meal in Europe, he averred that 'there [were] few Englishmen who have eaten a fricassé of the thighs of this animal in France or Italy [that] would wish to do so again'.[4] In 1860, the *Athenæum* came out in favour of frogs. 'There is no reason', it remarked, 'why we should eschew frogs, and relish turtle'. But notwithstanding this logic, *The Epicure's Year Book* for 1868 admitted that, alas, 'the poorest [English] man would disdain to eat a single pair' of frogs' legs.[5] A few cookery books from the same era attempted to convince the English household to essay the dish, but without much hope.

Even the great chef Marie-Antonin Carême (1784–1833) conceded that the frog was not to everyone's taste. And, strangely, even for this fan of the *grenouille* it seemed necessary to point out those whose consumption of the animal was beyond the pale. Carême unfavourably compared the Viennese appetite for the whole animal with the preference of the French for the thighs alone, implying that there was something distasteful about the former. Carême wrote a number of recipes for frogs' legs, frying them, and especially making them into soups and bouillons (one recipe calls for six dozen thighs – quite a demanding requirement).[6]

Although frogs were to become signifiers of the fashionable new *haute cuisine* by the late nineteenth century, Carême's early nineteenth-century dishes were very much inspired by the frog's traditional health-giving properties; his recommendation of frog bouillon for curing consumptive coughs reached all the way back to the remedies of Pliny the Elder. References to French frog-eating date back to the Middle Ages, but another celebrated chef, Georges Auguste Escoffier (1846–1935), traced their widespread consumption to a sixteenth-century entrepreneur from the Auvergne region who made his fortune selling them to Parisians. (The fact that this astute merchant only recommended the legs for eating supposedly meant that he sold even more.) Escoffier was apparently peeved at the refusal of the English to countenance eating his national delicacy and so, in 1908, he planned a batrachian deception on no less a figure than the Prince of Wales. Engaged to prepare a buffet for a *grande soirée* at the Savoy, he included *cuisses de nymphes à l'Aurore* (thighs of dawn nymphs) among the many dishes on offer to the guests, revealing only afterwards their true nature. Amused and impressed, Prince Edward ordered some more nymphs a few days later. Escoffier was apparently chided for the suggestiveness of his dish's title, but he stood fast (excusing himself with a slightly different version of the story, whereby a beautiful hostess had asked him to disguise the nature of the dish to spare her guests' sensibilities). *Nymphes à l'Aurore* – without their salacious *cuisses* – live on in the latest edition of Escoffier's *Guide Culinaire*. To prepare them, poach the frogs' legs in white wine, and set them in champagne-flavoured fish aspic. *Délicieuses*.[7]

Thus the *haute cuisine* frog has an international history, created as a gourmet dish in England by the French. The historical complexities of sibling nationalism – the cultural politics of envy and suspicion – have led to the edible frog's strange dual status as a dish that is both desired and reviled, its national hybridity unacknowledged on either side of the Channel. Since Escoffier's time, many great French chefs at home and abroad have continued to create and refine dishes involving frogs. La Grenouille in New York (f. 1962) pays homage to the ingredient in its name – a signifier of its sophistication and, by association with French cuisine, its excellence. Much as in the early nineteenth century, fashionable Anglo-American eaters today esteem the frog, while the popular taste remains somewhat more sceptical.

La Grenouille's chef imports his frogs' legs all the way from France, but down in French-influenced New Orleans, where frogs are a far more popular dish than up north, the American bullfrog, *Rana catesbeiana*, substitutes for the European *R. esculenta* on the dinner table. However, the biggest exporter of frogs' legs today is Indonesia, which along with other East Asian countries uses the Indian bullfrog, *Hoplobatrachus tigerinus*, widely in its cuisine.[8] Indonesia alone exported over four million kilograms of frogs' legs in 2009.[9] Breeders prevent the meat from tasting too gamey for Western palates by feeding the frogs a bland diet, preventing their natural consumption of bugs and vertebrates.

What is at the root of Anglo-American disgust at the notion of eating frogs? Fish are just as slimy, after all. Following Eco's definition of ugliness, a 'lack of equilibrium, in the organic relationship between the parts of the whole', we might suppose that it is the inharmonious combination of limbs – associated with mammals – and slime – associated with fish and the primordial generally – that is to blame.[10] My hunch is that Anglo-American ideas about proper eating are also reliant on a tacit, internalized version of the great chain of nature. Proper foodstuffs are found further down the chain, not across it. Thus, most of the meats consumed in Britain and America are naturally (or thought so to be) herbivorous. The thought of eating another meat-eater is wrong; eating a herbivorous frog is one thing, but eating an Indian bullfrog that has just eaten a mouse – a mammal, like us! – is abhorrent. And if eating across the chain of nature is wrong, then cannibalism is off the scale. The zoologist Edward Bartlett (1836–1908) was horrified to see an American bullfrog (*R. catesbeiana*) in his keeping consume several of his European cousins, the 'pretty fire-bellied toad' (*Bombinator igneus*). 'Our Yankee frog commenced immediately to swallow "alive and kicking" the unfortunate Saxony toads', he reported. Adding comic horror to the situation was Bartlett's impression that the frog's distended jaw reminded him of 'kind mothers who say to the baby, "I could eat you, you darling"'.[11] It is an amusing story, but I confess that I would baulk somewhat at seeing this and then eating the bullfrog – an edible species – in question. It may be that eating too far down the chain of nature is also taboo; hence, even frogs with more harmless diets are, like insects, too far removed from mammals to be considered for edibility. (Actually, although *Rana esculenta* does not have a reputation for grotesque consumption like *R. catesbeiana*, scientists have found that it does possess cannibalistic tendencies.)

Contrary to popular belief, the Anglo-American tendency to refer to the French as frogs is not, or not entirely, due to their presumed eating habits. The story starts out entirely differently, in the Middle Ages. Alas, as historian Michael Randall explains, the French seem to have brought the slur upon themselves by unwisely – and possibly uniquely – attempting to forge an affirmative identification with batrachians.[12]

At the birth of the French legend, the toad had its usual evil characteristics. A popular fourteenth-century history told how King Clovis, prior to his conversion to Christianity, had three toads on his coat of arms. Thanks to a miraculous intervention, these *males bestes* were transformed overnight into pure, Christian lilies (*fleurs de lis*), marking the beginning of Clovis's successful Christian reign. During the sixteenth century, however, ideals of kingship changed. It became important to recognize the king's absolute power: to show that Clovis had exhibited sovereign quality even before his conversion. He could not be an unwise man who became a good king thanks only to a miracle. Thus, the representation of the toad had to change; Clovis must have chosen it, even before conversion, for a good reason. 'It is in the nature of the toad', explained one sixteenth-century historian,

Frogs at the Latona Fountain in the gardens of the Palace of Versailles.

'to find always for himself the best, the most fertile, and the most useful place. And it is for this reason the king of France possesses and occupies the best, the most fertile and the most useful land in the world'. Another sixteenth-century historian substituted a tree frog for the toad on Clovis's pre-conversion coat of arms – slightly less problematic, less demonic, in terms of its connotations for Clovis and French notions of kingship.

For a while, the PR job performed on the toad-king by six-teenth-century French historians seemed to hold, until after about 50 or 100 years, when they began to downplay or even deny the legend altogether. Unfortunately, however, the story was out – to the delight of the foes of France. It has been suggested that frogs were used in England to lampoon the French as early as 1580, when the folk song 'Frog Went A-courting' was popularized: supposedly it was a satirical account of the attempt by Francis, Duke of Anjou, to woo Elizabeth I. By the seventeenth century, for certain, enemies of the French were exploiting their toadish connections with glee. The Flemish were particularly merciless in this respect. They began to call the French toads and their king the 'descendant of toads'; Dutch histories of France deliberately mis-drew the contemporary French coat of arms with toads on it. Edward Topsell, in his pro-Protestant *History of Serpents*, also repeated the legend of Clovis to the detriment of the French.

Historian David Bindman has discovered that during the later seventeenth and eighteenth centuries, the French were turning the slur the other way; along with the English they began portraying the Dutch as frogs, for the ostensible reason that they lived in a low-lying and swampy land.[13] Dutch peasants in particular were pictured in anuran form, as fat, lazy and cunning. One particularly sophisticated satire of 1672 showed 'Holland . . . as a huge horse turd' and the Dutch as 'frogs who grow from maggots feeding on it'.

Following the Glorious Revolution of 1688, when the Dutch William III took the English throne, inhabitants of the Netherlands dropped out of the satirical sights of the British. Their place was taken by the Catholic French, and by those foppish Englishmen and women who imitated them. A crucial failing of the French was their insincere and fancy sense of taste, characterized above all by their preference for silly little servings of food rather than good platefuls of 'honest' beef: 'In foreign vests the gaudy Fops may shine,/ And on dissected frogs politely dine.'

As the eighteenth century went on, the eating of frogs 'became a sign less of luxury and affected delicacy than of poverty'. Hogarth's 1756 engraving *The Invasion* showed thin French soldiers mustering in Calais, dreaming of England's rich foods while preparing a paltry kebab of frogs for themselves. Similarly, Isaac Cruikshank's etching *French Happiness, English Misery* (1793) compared fat Englishmen enjoying their meat with a group of scrawny, post-Revolutionary Frenchmen grasping at a single frog. Soon after Cruikshank made his drawing,

AMSTERDAM in a Dam'd Predicament,— or— The last Scene of the Republican Pantomine.

French Happiness   *English Misery*

the Napoleonic Wars produced an absolute proliferation of English representations of the impoverished, frog-eating French. To Bindman's focus on poverty we could also add that frogs were a signifier of Catholicism. Frogs were recommended both as a health-giving sustenance freely available to the poor invalid, and as a meat that might be eaten during Lent, since they were closer to fish than to other quadrupeds. They had little blood, and much phlegm, and were unlikely to arouse the passions.[14]

By the nineteenth century, with Dutch power in abeyance, the French resumed their batrachian characterization and completed their metamorphosis from frog-eaters to frogs pure and simple. Political allegories concerning frogs had a lot to do with this transition. In Aesop's fable, the frogs demand a king but later come to regret it when he – a crane or a crocodile, depending on the version told – begins to eat them. The propensity of the French to revolt – and like Aesop's subjects, to end up with a worse regime than they had before – therefore completed their identity with frogs in the light of this tale.[15] There is another Aesopian frog connection, 'The Ox and the Frog', in which the frog attempts to puff himself up to the size of the former, until he unfortunately bursts. Victorian British satirists recounted this fable, casting the ox as a British bull, and Louis VIII, pretender to the English throne, as the fatally conceited frog.[16]

In more recent history, the French have been joined by other nationalities in their derogatory association with the frog. During the Second World War, British propaganda portrayed the Japanese as toads. More recent British enemies have been in the Middle East; as the British public assimilated the notion of the previously demonized Iraqis becoming allies in 2006, the *Daily Mail* newspaper reflected the difficulty of that transition by reporting that 'Iraqi soldiers bit the heads off

James Gillray, 'Amsterdam in a Dam'd Predicament; or, The Last Scene of the Republican Pantomime', 1787, hand-coloured etching. The Dutch were widely caricatured as frogs in the seventeenth century, as this print shows.

Isaac Cruikshank's etching *French Happiness, English Misery* of 1793 is an early example of the Anglo-American association of frogs with the French.

frogs . . . at a ceremony to transfer Najaf province from US to Iraqi control'. The Iraqis' execution of this repugnant batrachian ritual signalled their doubtfulness even when in an official state of alliance. Some three years earlier, shortly before the commencement of the war, the *Independent* newspaper gave another twist on the politicized frog in its cartoon 'Toadies say: hop off frogs!' The French Foreign Minister had come out against the proposed invasion of Iraq but his British equivalent, Jack Straw, followed the hawkish US line in condemning the French stance. In Dave Brown's cartoon, the frogness of the French is ironically referenced by portraying Straw as a toad. As a toad(y) of Bush, it suggests, Straw is more despicable than the much-despised French frogs.

When frogs get out of place, as 'invasive species', they become a focus for these issues of nation, ethnicity and identity. The best-known example of this phenomenon is the cane toad (*Bufo marinus*) in Australia, a large species whose most substantial recorded example weighed in at 2.65 kg.[17] In 1935, the Queensland scientist Reginald Mungomery collected 102 cane toads

Aesop's fable of the crane and frogs, illustrated in a 19th-century wood engraving after Gustave Doré.

from an experimental colony in Honolulu to take back home. He had seen the toads demonstrated at a conference in Puerto Rico, controlling beetle pests of sugar cane; Mungomery hoped that they would do the same for the Australian Greyback Cane Beetle. Warning bells should, arguably, have rung when he bagged his first 50 in only one hour. This was too easy; the toads had already spread all over the island and begun to plague local gardens.

Back in Australia, the imported specimens produced 42,000 more adult toads for release within one year. Local farmers were initially anxious for their land to be selected for toad settlement, but before very long it became apparent that the toads were of no use for their intended purpose. Some blamed this on the fact that the greyback beetle, unlike the Puerto Rican beetle, did not return regularly to ground where the toads could get at them. Subsequent commentators have argued that the reduction in Puerto Rican beetles during the toad trial was actually a coincidence, and that unusual weather conditions – not the toads – were the cause of what in any case turned out to be a temporary reduction in beetle numbers.

Human and ecological concerns about the toads' release were expressed as far back as the year of the policy's introduction, and faced with these the Australian government temporarily halted their release. Mungomery's bullish insistence won through, however, and the ban was soon reversed. Within a very short space of time, the critics' concerns were vindicated, and the disastrous effects of the toads began to become evident. *B. marinus* feeds voraciously, destroying native insect, bird, mammalian and reptilian life. It is highly noxious and the few native snakes that attempt to prey on it are poisoned. (Meat ants have recently been discovered to be a notable exception to this rule, and appear to predate effectively on young toads.) Mungomery himself remained unrepentant, continuing to view his task with almost megalomaniac zeal.

Cane toads continue to spread inexorably across Australia from their original introduction point in the northeast, at a rate of over 100 km per year. They are proving suited to all environments, including semi-arid areas and in water of up to 15 per cent salinity, and now occupy well over a million square kilometres of land. Some ecologists have questioned the extent to which *B. marinus* poses a threat to biodiversity; some habitats and some species, it seems, are more damaged by the toads than others. Nevertheless, millions of Australian dollars have been spent trying to halt the toads' progress and to eradicate them where they have already arrived.

With typical Aussie bravado, some Australians have adopted the cane toad as a kind of mascot. In general, however, they are loathed. Attracted by garbage and lights (that in turn attract insects), large numbers of toads swagger into gardens and houses. Pets that investigate them too closely will die of the potent venom in their skin. Unavoidable on the highways, they burst under car wheels and splatter their guts across the roads. Ecologists and geographers, as well as historians of science, have noted the nature of the military and nationalistic language that is invariably used to articulate this disgust and dismay: a vocabulary of 'invasion', and of 'alien' and 'native' species. Critics point out the implicitly xenophobic connotations of this language, and also the illogic of treating humans and animals in different ways when it comes to discussing migration and colonization. All organisms once had to colonize the area in which they now live, and many in their evolutionary past have come some distance to do so, or (like the toad with its human vector) have done so in conjunction with other organisms. So why pick out recent colonists as somehow unnatural?

In the case of the cane toad in Australia, this critical reading seems plausible. This is an instance of an immigrant population – and one with a poor record in regard to the indigenous population at that – getting extremely upset about another immigrant invader. Australian politics has more recently also been exercised with human immigrants; in 1992, a policy of mandatory detention of unauthorized immigration arrivals was established, and in 1997, the far-right One Nation Party made anti-immigration policies central to its manifesto. So, one might be tempted to posit that what we have here is a projection onto the toads, on the part of the white colonists, of a selfish concern that no one else should usurp their colonization. Alternatively, it might conceivably be read as a displacement of the colonists' guilt at having done much the same thing as the toad.

Or could it just be that the toads are really and simply nasty? I must confess frankly that I would be horrified and disgusted to have an evening on the patio spoiled by giant hopping toads, or worse still by encountering them indoors. Counting in favour of actual nastiness, one might note that even those with impeccable liberal qualities find the toads repulsive; although in keeping with their world-view they may class the phenomenon not so much as invasion as an example of the 'McDonaldization of the biosphere'. On the other hand, as Tim Low reminds us, Australians are ignorant of the vast majority of introduced species to their country, many of which have proved considerably more harmful than the toad. Other introduced species are 'nice' and have been given a kind of honorary native status: olives, honeybees and trout, to name but three. Thus, the toad *is* doing some kind of special representative work.

What is it about toads, as opposed to other animals? Finding six woodlice in the house would not bother me at all. Finding half a dozen feral cats would be perturbing but not revolting.

We could here consider a genuine historical counterfactual along similar lines; in 1902, moles were proposed for introduction into Australia as a means to control insect pests. Had this been followed through, and even if they had disrupted Australian ecologies, it is hard to imagine them provoking such disgust. Irritation, perhaps, but not disgust. As in the case of eating frogs, Eco's definition of formal ugliness – as disequilibrium in the natural pattern – again works to a certain extent as an explanation for the toads' effect. In this instance, the toad represents a disruption in the expected number of batrachians, and also in size compared to the European norm. The latter is also true of the American bullfrog, which has recently been identified as a problem in the UK. 'The bullies of the frog world [have] crossed the Atlantic', warned the *Independent* in 2000, at just the time

The American bullfrog (*Rana catesbeiana*) is a recent invasive species in the UK.

that anti-American sentiment was running high among Brits. In some senses, then, there are inherent or at least long-established attributes of the frog that make cane toads and American bullfrogs such targets of loathing – slime, warts, poison and so on. However, their being out of place is a significant factor, and it seems probable that they are the focus for some xenophobic sentiment. As in all cases where frogs are used to demarcate between 'them and us', their unpleasant features – both natural and cultural – have become mutually reinforcing.

4 Under the Knife

In 1847, the young surgeon Hermann von Helmholtz was, by his own account, 'waiting impatiently for the spring'. One might be forgiven for thinking that he had love on his mind; his engagement was to be announced only a month or two later. But, in fact, he was thinking about frogs. Specifically, he was waiting for the frogs of Potsdam to emerge from their winter hiding places and venture forth to breed by the ponds. At that moment he would be able to take his collecting jars and capture them in their dozens before transporting them back to his laboratory. Helmholtz had some nasty things in store for the little creatures; they were, in his own words, 'those old martyrs of science'.

Helmholtz was neither the first nor the last person to experiment on frogs. One of the earliest hi-tech pieces of science, Robert Boyle's air pump (1659), was used for the purpose. It comprised a chamber that could be emptied of air, creating a perfect vacuum, and almost immediately experimenters tried frogs and toads (among other animals) to see how long they could survive inside.

'Hey, let's try it with a frog!' The same experimental method quickly occurred to twentieth- and twenty-first-century scientists working with high field magnets, a contemporary example of apparatus as impressive and complex as Boyle's was in its day. Inside the device, the atoms of the animal act as tiny magnets

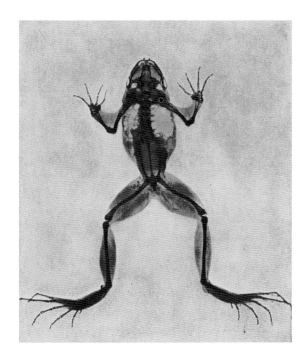

and are repelled by the powerful magnet of the machine. In a lightweight organism, this force of repulsion is sufficient to counteract gravity and the frog levitates freely as though floating and turning in space. 'The small frog looked comfortable inside the magnet and, afterwards, happily joined its fellow frogs in a biology department', reported Dutch experimenters.[1] Frogs and tadpoles have also been sent into space. Initial Soviet attempts to raise tadpoles in space – which seem to have been at the speculative end of science – were only 'marginally successful'. Other attempts have been more focused in purpose. In 1970, NASA launched two American bullfrogs in their 'Orbiting Frog Otolith' to understand how the human inner ear might respond

An experimental frog levitates in a high field magnet.

to long periods of weightlessness. More recent experiments have aimed to understand how tadpoles deal with the water-based gravitational challenges of real life. The scientists behind these latest experiments wonder whether tadpoles can 'learn' to live in zero gravity.

A great deal of early anatomical and physiological work with animals was inspired by a desire to understand the human body, and so frogs, much farther removed from us than mammals, were not initially an especially popular choice for experimentation. Perhaps the earliest researcher to make significant use of frogs was Jan Swammerdam (1637–1680), a Dutchman who is best known today for his microscopy and anatomy.

Swammerdam put frogs in what is, from today's perspective, a surprising category. They formed a part of his *Natural History of Insects* (1669). This was later expanded as *The Bible of Nature* (*c*. 1679).[2] In it, Swammerdam aimed to show that 'all God's works are governed by the same rules'.[3] Swammerdam used frogs as an in-between animal, standing midway between insects and the 'larger, or sanguiferous animals', to show that all were part of the same pattern of creation.

Swammerdam's first staging post in this strategy was to show that the development of insect larvae and tadpoles proceeded in the same way. Swammerdam was an extraordinarily talented dissector and microscopist, and his skills were well suited to the task. Yet demonstrating that frogs developed according to the same law as insects was not enough, for it merely reduced the frogs – never a high-status animal in any case – to that of insects. So, Swammerdam next took a clever turn in his *Bible of Nature*, relating the frogs to the higher animals. Until this time, research on muscular movements had been largely carried out on cats,

One of the frogs used in an embryology experiment on the Spacelab-J flight launched by the Space Shuttle *Endeavor*, 1992.

Jan Swammerdam was one of the first natural philosophers to experiment extensively on frogs. From Swammerdam's *Bible of Nature* (1679; published 1737).

dogs and poultry. Typically, their nerves were exposed and stimulated with all manner of things: pins, scalpels, heat and caustic or 'acrid liquors'. What Swammerdam did was to try these experiments instead upon frogs. Swammerdam found that the frog's body was not required whole to produce the effect. A nerve-muscle preparation dissected out of a frog, when touched with scissors or other instruments, also strongly contracted.

Swammerdam was quite explicit that 'experiments on the particular motion of the muscles in the Frog . . . may be also, in general, applied to all the motions of the muscles in Men and Brutes'. One might perhaps think that this was a rather radical conclusion – placing humans in the same category as animals – but Swammerdam drew a devout lesson from his findings. The frog's assistance in Godly reflection was wonderfully indicated by its 'wonderful copulation', in which the male 'most beautifully joins his toes between one another, in the same manner as people do their fingers at prayers'.[4] From the insect to the frog, and from the frog to the human; the whole of God's creation was now joined in one seamless, law-like continuity.

In the eighteenth century, the Italian priest and investigator Lazzaro Spallanzani (1729–1799) continued the quest into understanding the body, employing an extraordinary and inventive cruelty to frogs to do so. He cut off their legs to see if they would re-grow (they did, if the specimens were young enough); he tried different ways of killing them by suffocation and a pin through the brain (they all worked); and abused male toads and frogs during the act of mating to see if he could induce them to let go (even decapitation would not do the trick).

Spallanzani's heartless science was a long way from certain frog studies carried out by the British traveller and naturalist Robert Townson (1762–1827). During a visit to central Europe in 1793, Townson acquired a female tree frog (*Rana arborea*), which he then proceeded to keep in a little box in his pocket. He named her Musidora, from the Greek 'gift of the muses': presumably a reference to her musical utterances, common to the species as a whole. As historian Christopher Plumb notes, the sounds of the beautiful little frog – 'much like a blunt file against a piece of steel' – were more pleasing to some than others.[5] Plumb describes how Townson cared for his little frog, keeping her in a glass of water by the window of his Göttingen study. In this warm room she lived through three winters without the hibernation usual to frogs, and grew tame enough to sit in Townson's hand, where he fed her on flies. Townson's scientific observations on amphibians made numerous reference to Musidora by name, and it was with great sorrow that he announced in one such publication:

> I am exceedingly sorry to [inform] Musidora's friends (for she had many) that she is no more. She sickened soon

Robert Townson's pet Musidora (*c.* 1791–4) was a European tree frog like this (*Hyla arborea*, then known as *Rana arborea*).

after she reached Great Britain, and died in the night of 25th of June 1794.[6]

Yet, notwithstanding his fondness for Musidora, Townson conducted crueller experiments on her conspecifics, of which he kept up to 80 in his basement. He was inspired in his researches by the fact that nobody appeared to have understood frog respiration, merely – and inappropriately – generalizing its nature from other animals. In a strange kind of way, even his cruel experiments were perhaps bred of a fondness, or rather respect for, the frog.

The best known of all eighteenth-century frogs belonged to Spallanzani's contemporary, the anatomist Luigi Galvani (1737–1798). There are several variants on the myth that tells the story of Galvani, the lightning and the frog. The most touching version has Galvani in his kitchen, preparing a meal of frogs' legs for his wife Lucia, unwell in bed. As he chops the skinned legs, he accidentally touches his knife across from the muscle to the nerve, provoking the leg to kick. Another version has Galvani cutting frogs up for experiment, when distant lightning causes the legs to kick; another still has Lucia back in the picture (this time healthy) and noticing for herself the electrical machine nearby that is the cause of the leg's kicking.

Most people are so excited to get on to the electricity part of the story that they forget to ask what the frogs were doing on Galvani's bench in the first place. Vivisecting a frog to the point where it would respond to electricity was no simple task, and certainly not something that could be done casually or accidentally. By the mid-eighteenth century, it had become commonplace to ascribe the nervous stimulation of muscle, such as Swammerdam had observed, to the action of electricity. The phenomenon of electricity had been identified earlier in the century, and in addition to its theoretical role in muscular movement, it was associated with medical practices whereby patients received shocks intended to improve or restore their health. Yet despite these theories and practices, there was little by way of substantial evidence that the two were connected: that 'animal spirits' were actually electrical in nature. Thus it was in the late 1770s that Galvani began, in somewhat the same spirit as Swammerdam,

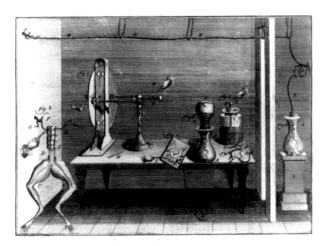

to explore the irritability of nerves, and to attempt to forge a direct connection between nerves and electricity.

Because the frog's muscle contracted when it was connected to the nerve by metal, Galvani considered that his hypothesis – that frogs contained animal electricity – was confirmed. The electrical fluid existed in a state of disequilibrium (condensed in the nerves, and rarefied in muscle), and was conveyed from one region to the other by the metal, producing a contraction. Galvani's conclusion was, however, met with disbelief by the physicist Alessandro Volta (1745–1827). Volta attempted to repeat Galvani's experiment, and claimed that he could do so only if he used a bridge that was composed of two metals; it was the metals that were causing the jerk, not the frog. Volta's ultimate rebuttal was to create a pile of moist metallic bodies, making an electric battery from two different types of metal – no frog was needed. This was widely considered, by physicists at least, to put paid to Galvani's ideas. Whereas Galvani treated the organic body as a topic in its own right, Volta treated the

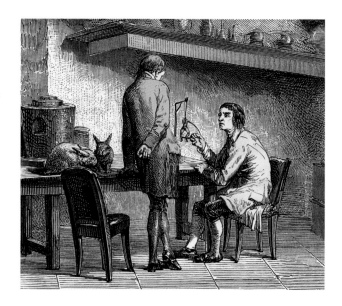

Jean Noel Halle and Alexander von Humboldt experimenting on frogs (1798). The rabbits may get a lucky escape thanks to the sacrificial frog.

frog as a piece of physical apparatus, and an unreliable one at that. Inorganic equipment was much more decisive for himself and his followers.

Despite the 'disproof' of Volta, many dozens if not hundreds of frogs were used in electrical experiments by physiologists over the next century, and the man who really started the trend was the German Johannes Müller (1801–1858). Müller was trying to confirm the work of François Magendie (1783–1855), who had claimed to show that nerves from different roots did different things, those joining the spine at the front controlling movement, and those joining it at the back relaying sensation (which in an experimental context meant pain). Magendie's experiments were carried out on live dogs, but when Müller tried replicating them on rabbits, he found that the creatures' general distress was so great that it was impossible to discern the results of stimulating particular nerves. So, at some time in the 1820s or early 1830s, Müller hit upon the idea of using frogs instead.

Like Swammerdam, Müller found it comparatively easy to expose the spinal cord, and similarly noted the frog's 'tenacious' grip on life, meaning that its nerves and muscles continued to respond to irritation for a long time on the laboratory bench – up to 30 hours, compared with fifteen minutes in cats and dogs. Müller was so pleased with his results that he encouraged aspiring young physiologists to go and do likewise. His students, the friends Emil Du Bois-Reymond (1818–1896) and Hermann von Helmholtz (1821–1894), took him at his word.

Physically, the frog was indispensable to the questions these men wanted to explore. Helmholtz, for example, wanted to find out whether muscles observed the law of the conservation of energy: when they contracted, did all the heat generated come from their own, internal chemical reactions? To do this, he had to find a muscle that would work in isolation from its normal blood supply, otherwise the results would be muddied by the muscle burning oxygen from incoming blood. Only the muscles of cold-blooded animals could survive in this condition for any length of time, making the frog an ideal animal to use. Meanwhile, for Du Bois-Reymond the frog's leg was simply the most sensitive galvanometer that he could find. He almost drove himself crazy trying to create an artificial device that responded to a current as low as the frog's leg did, eventually succeeding by making an unimaginably tedious 24,160 turns in a thin wire coil.

Working with frogs presented many practical challenges. Even when dead, the frogs made certain demands of the physiologists in order to go on working for them. Historian Laura Otis describes all of this wonderfully well.[7] There were no dedicated laboratories for the work of the physiologists, and so Du

Bois-Reymond had to experiment in his room at his parents' house, and at the Anatomical Museum in Berlin. His parents' neighbours objected to his filling the house with animals for experiment, and dogs were absolutely out of the question (suggesting, perhaps, a more pragmatic reason why he switched to anurans). Frogs were just about acceptable, although one wonders what they thought of the numbers; by autumn 1841, 100 frogs were sharing his room.

Obtaining the frogs was difficult. Du Bois-Reymond depended upon a supply sent to him by train from Leipzig, if necessary bribing the conductor to make sure they reached him before they expired. Events conspired to disrupt his supply; while the rest of Berlin was in revolutionary upheaval in April 1848, Du Bois-Reymond complained to his supplier about the 'lack of frogs'. Looking after the frogs was also tricky. During four successive winters in the 1840s, Du Bois-Reymond lost 10–50 per cent of his frogs to disease. On another occasion, all his frogs froze to death, due to the thoughtless absence of his servant. A final challenge was presented by the need to transport the frogs and their corpses between the Anatomical Museum and his parents' house. Du Bois-Reymond had to come and go between the two frequently, carrying 'a sack of frogs and ice' in the heat of the day.

The odd thing is that although Müller and his disciples were utterly dependent on frogs for their research, forced to confront them in all their bodily reality, they did their best to deny their animality – to reduce them to mere instruments – in the story of their science. As Otis explains, the careers of these men were embedded in debates about vitalism. Vitalism, the idea that there was something scientifically special about living bodies, was associated with eighteenth-century romantic philosophy, and tended to be espoused by the politically conservative.

Anti-vitalists, who tended to be politically progressive, insisted that the physical processes of living organisms were no different to those found in a test tube. As anti-vitalists, Du Bois-Reymond and Helmholtz had to distance themselves from their animals – to make it clear that their science was not specially the study of life.

In his account of Müller's life, Du Bois-Reymond made his master's story one of death and resurrection, a messianic triumph over the 'dragon' of vitalism. He ascribed Müller's 1827 breakdown to the heroic but draining self-experimentation that he had been carrying out, trying his best to defeat the dragon. Müller's adoption of the frog, 'forgotten' since Galvani's day, was the turning point according to Du Bois-Reymond. The evil dragon was slain, thanks to the batrachian victim sacrificed in Müller's new experiments. (Or, as in the evolution of the frog king story, the medieval dragon was replaced with the harmless nineteenth-century frog.) The sacrificed frog now had to surrender for a second time, disappearing from the science so as not to give the impression that the latter was intrinsically rooted in the study of living things: to prove that the science was not vitalist. And Du Bois-Reymond absolutely had to lose the jokey title ascribed to him by his friends at the Anatomy Museum, 'the frog doctor'. Thus the experiments of Du Bois-Reymond and Helmholtz now take their place in retrospective histories of both physiology and physics, but the frogness of their frogs has been almost completely lost. The anuran has been reduced to a mere instrument.

Meanwhile, in Britain there was a growing sense of unease about animal experimentation. In its founding statement of 1824, the SPCA (Society for the Prevention of Cruelty to Animals) singled out vivisection as a practice to which it was opposed. One should not overstate the extent of this moral outrage, but nevertheless criticism was present, targeted particularly at foreign researchers. In response to this groundswell of opinion, British physiologists began to choose cold-blooded animals for their work whenever they could; intuitively, they were less distressing to work on.

Among these physiologists was Marshall Hall (1790–1857), whose scientific aims included proving that the brain was the centre of all sensation, and that only insensate reflexes existed in decerebrated frogs. Hall had a number of prominent critics who insisted that consciousness extended into the spinal cord, and combined with the general public distaste at animal experimentation this prompted Hall to defend his practices. Hall emphasized that the use of vivisection should be minimized, and that where necessary it should always be carried out on the lowest possible type of creature. He suggested that frogs were especially good animals to use; their low position on the zoological scale was proved by the fact that they continued to exhibit the phenomena of life after mutilation – even decapitation. As lower animals, they were also less able to feel pain.

Concerns about animal vivisection were coming to a head in 1870 when Darwin's great publicist, T. H. Huxley (1825–1895), borrowed Hall's frog in his lecture 'Has a Frog a Soul?' Huxley's short answer to his own question was: no. To get there, he drew on Hall's experiments. Huxley's *ad absurdum* argument described how ever-smaller parts of the frog could be dissected out of the animal but would still respond to stimuli. Either metaphysical possibility – that the soul, too, was chopped up in this process, or that it somehow hung in the ether connecting the separate parts of the frog – was ridiculous.

It appears rather odd that Huxley should be debating the matter of the soul as late as 1870, by which time it had completely dropped off the agenda of serious physiological research – a straw man. Moreover, Huxley signally failed to address a much more important contemporary question in his lecture, namely, whether the frog had *consciousness*. This was a significant absence, for just at this time anti-vivisectionists were arguing that animals' consciousness of pain made them morally unacceptable subjects for live experimentation. The 1876 Cruelty to Animals Act turned upon precisely the question of animal consciousness, insisting that all vivisected vertebrates should be anaesthetized to prevent the sensation of pain. No doubt Huxley's lecture was in large part, like so much of his lecturing, anti-theist grandstanding. But by dismissing the question of consciousness and focusing instead on the 'enlightenment' of experiment, it was also an attempt to assert the right of biologists to continue using live frogs and other animals in their work.

The best-known experiment with frogs is perhaps also the cruellest: a frog plunged in boiling water, so it is said, will hop out, but a frog placed in a vessel of cold water and heated slowly will stay put and perish. This factoid serves many purposes. Herpetologist Whit Gibbons of the University of Georgia recalls hearing a Mississippi Baptist preach on the topic, using it as an example of how 'gradual habituation to a devilish situation leads to acceptance of an even worse one'. Al Gore used the metaphor in similar fashion in his documentary *An Inconvenient Truth*, to suggest that humans might go on accepting gradual climate change until it is too late. In September 2009, Fox News's Glenn Beck employed the frog in another of its frequently used senses, to capture the perceived bit-by-bit erosion of civil liberties by the federal government. A video of him apparently placing a frog in a pot of boiling water to illustrate this point was swiftly placed on the Internet, forcing him to explain in a subsequent show that the experiment was faked. Beck evidently enjoyed 'frog gate', as he called it, which for him was further illustration of the foolish liberal sensitivities that he was trying to highlight in the first place.

The 'myth' has, in fact, rather strong historical roots in reality. In the 1870s, boiling frogs was a popular pastime for physiologists, although they were not always precisely agreed on why the activity was a useful one. Upon reading accounts of these experiments, the fact that immediately strikes one is that, in most of them, the frogs have had their brains removed. Thus, Friedrich Goltz reported in 1869:

> A normal frog if immersed in water which is gradually heated, speedily becomes violent in his attempts to escape. In striking contrast to this phenomenon is the behaviour of the brainless frog, which . . . sits motionless until it is dead from the excessive heat.[8]

To the modern reader, this observation appears to be one of Swiftian asininity. A frog lacking its brain is hardly thinking straight. To make sense of why the result seemed significant, we need to understand what the frog had become for physiologists. We have already seen an example of how the frog was considered as a set of qualities that could then be projected in their purest form onto another carrier; for the early modern Edward Topsell, frogs were a collection of unpleasant characteristics, and the ultimate frog was a toad, in the sense that it possessed all the key qualities of the frog to a purer and greater degree. Now, for nineteenth-century physiologists, the frog had become a piece of mechanical apparatus for answering a series of physiological questions about nerves and muscles. Their über-frog was one in which the brain had been removed, allowing its nervous responses to be seen still more plainly and in their most automatic state, uncomplicated by higher-level cerebral processes.

As one researcher put it, 'the frog . . . is now admitted to be to a great extent a reflex mechanism; . . . the brainless frog [is] a much more perfect reflex apparatus than the normal one'.[9] This conception of the frog was so well-established that at least two independent lines of batrachian-cooking experiment were commenced without their authors knowing about one another's work.

Goltz's discovery was surprising to his contemporary physiologists for at least two reasons. The one that concerned the American William Sedgwick was to do with the general properties of nerves and muscles at different temperatures; Sedgwick expected a period of increased activity in the frog's nervous system before heat rigor set in, but Goltz did not report this. Others were interested that decerebrated frogs showed no response to heat in particular, since they displayed quite co-ordinated and complex responses to other types of stimuli.

Still another approach to the phenomenon came from the German physiologist A. Heinzmann, who speculated that the dying frog demonstrated a general property of nerves. He suggested that if the intensity of nerve stimulation were started small enough, and increased gradually enough, then it might be increased in intensity until it destroyed the nerve without ever provoking a muscular reaction (because the muscle was waiting for some kind of sudden step-change in the nervous action before it responded). He found that even a normal frog would stay put if the water were heated slowly enough.

In his 1897 book, *The New Psychology*, Edward Wheeler Scripture reported Heinzmann's findings and added more: 'It has been found possible in $5\frac{1}{2}$ hours to actually crush a frog's foot without a sign that the pressure was felt by screwing down a button at the rate of 0.03 mm per minute.' Rather chillingly, he added: 'If a frog can be crushed or boiled without any evidence

A common frog (*Rana temporaria*) dissected to show various anatomical features, in George Rolleston's textbook *Forms of Animal Life* (1888). Frogs have been a mainstay of laboratory teaching since the late 19th century.

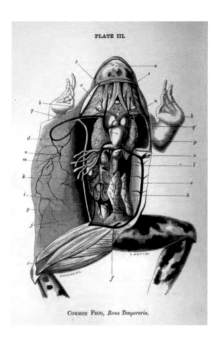

PLATE III.

COMMON FROG, *Rana Temporaria.*

that he has noticed it, it is at least an interesting question of what can be accomplished in this direction with human beings.'[10]

Leading biologists of the present day are anxious to dispel the 'myth' of the boiled frog. The Curator of Reptiles and Amphibians at the Smithsonian's National Museum of Natural History in Washington, DC, asserts with admirable firmness: 'Well that's, may I say, bullshit.'[11] These debunkers generally agree that frogs are way too jumpy to stay put anywhere, least of all in quite such an unpleasant environment. Yet at least two nineteenth-century experimenters really did think they had performed the feat of live-boiling, and it is unlikely that they were lying or totally incompetent. Perhaps the frogs were already dead when they were put in the water, or died some other way before it really

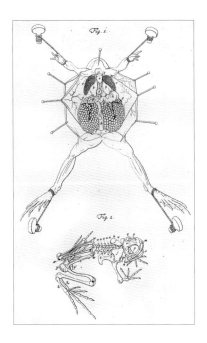

One of several illustrations of frog dissections in Roesel von Rosenhof's *Historia Naturalis Ranarum Nostratium* (1758).

heated up. Or perhaps they were placed in vessels from which it was actually not possible to jump. Another more subtle possibility comes in relation to the precise theories that experimenters were trying to prove. Their definitions of life and death were based upon particular understandings of nerve and muscle, and it may be that in looking for 'heat rigor' they were not thinking about life and death in the everyday sense. Hence, the decerebrated frog, which an ordinary person would definitely consider dead, was not dead for them.

This anxiety about the definition of death continues to leach into related anxieties about frog cruelty. When is a frog dead? When does dissection become vivisection? The reactive frog that was once celebrated for its tenacious hold on life must now,

for reasons of humaneness, be defined as dead. Decerebrated frogs are still used extensively by university-level students and lecturers in physiology: dead enough to feel no pain, but alive enough to respond to it. The preparation of these frogs is known as pithing; a needle is inserted near the top of the spinal column and moved around inside the skull so as to destroy the brain. The technique was developed as a means of slaughtering animals for consumption, but began to be used on frogs in the nineteenth century. It remains in use today, and has produced a seam of guilty humour about the frog's being 'pithed off' about its laboratory treatment.

In general, the scientific use of frogs, whether alive or dead, still fails to provoke as much criticism as the use of mammals, and anecdotal evidence suggests that herpetologists are not significant targets for animal rights activists. In 2008, Animal Aid protested that UK statistics for 2006 showed '12,459 amphibians were used in 20,616 procedures', and that 17,728 of these were without anaesthesia, even though 'amphibians are sentient beings capable of feeling stress and pain'.[12] The story raised little interest, however, and it is worth noting that procedures performed without anaesthetic may be done in this way precisely because they are quite harmless and pain-free for the frogs. Ecological herpetologists, who by and large care for frogs more than it is fashionable for a scientist to admit, complain that experimental restrictions are actually too tight. UK law, they say, prevents them from carrying out quite innocuous experiments (such as trying tadpoles in different kinds of pond water) by imposing disproportionate and onerous paperwork upon the process.

To date, six Nobel Prizes in physiology and medicine have resulted from investigations based exclusively on frogs, and there have been perhaps twice this number in which frogs played some role. Two Ig Nobel Prizes have also rewarded frogs. Whether used kindly or cruelly, frogs have been indispensable to a variety of experimental traditions throughout modern history.

5 Evolution on Fast-forward

In 1844, Robert Chambers – best known today for his dictionary – contemplated evolution by considering the frog. He imagined how frogspawn might appear to a mayfly during its brief 24 hours of life; it would have no idea of the drastic changes that were going to unfurl in their little, wriggly bodies, long after the mayfly itself was dead:

> Suppose that an ephemeron, hovering over a pool for its one April day of life, were capable of observing the fry of the frog in the water below. In its aged afternoon, having seen no change upon them for such a long time, it would be little qualified to conceive that the external branchiae [gills] of these creatures were to decay, and be replaced by internal lungs, that feet were to be developed, the tail erased, and the animal then to become a denizen of the land.[1]

Human beings, suggested Chambers, were in no less a state of ignorance when it came to nature around them: what appeared to be fixed species were, in the grand scheme of things, in a process of transformation from one form to another. Then as now, tadpoles and frogs are an almost irresistible image for the process so controversially described by Chambers. With gills

that turn into lungs, and legs that bud and grow to propel them from the water, it is as though they fast-forward through the slow evolutionary exodus from sea to land.

Of course, the frog is not in any literal sense a transitional organism between fish and mammals, but in the minds of many it has stood in that intermediary place. Older views of nature described a 'great chain' of lower to higher organisms; in 1849, for example, the Swiss-born American zoologist Louis Agassiz claimed that the development of the frog placed it between the fish and the reptile. When the great chain metaphor was given an evolutionary twist, the frog retained its place. Darwin, writing his *On the Origin of Species* (1859), knew that dissections of fish

Stufenfolge von dem Frosche bis zum Apollo-Profile.

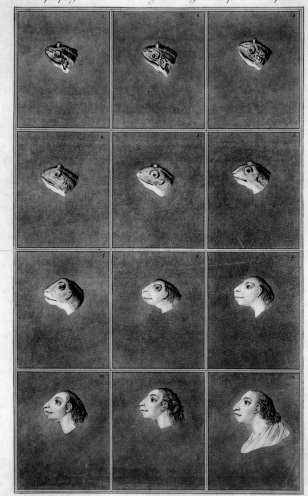

Ausgeführt und herausgegeben in Basel von Chr: von Mechel nach den Ideen des berühmten Lavaters.

and land animals by the comparative anatomist Richard Owen had already demonstrated that the swim bladders of fish were the 'same' as the lungs of land-living animals. Thus Darwin took it for granted that vertebrate life had begun in the water and subsequently moved onto the land. Frogs in this scheme too were 'between' fish and reptiles.

The very class Amphibia appears to owe its existence to evolutionary theory. Before Darwin, amphibians and reptiles were lumped together in a single class. In the authoritative edition of his *Systema Naturae* (1758), Linnaeus named the Amphibia as one of his four classes of vertebrates (alongside birds, mammals and fish). However, within the Amphibia, frogs and newts were grouped in the order of reptiles. In 1798, the great French comparative anatomist Georges Cuvier divided the vertebrates essentially the same way, but called the class that included frogs by the name of Linnaeus' order: 'reptiles'. Even Lamarck, an evolutionist and opponent of Cuvier, followed suit. Thus, although the word 'amphibian' was in use, it did not carry the imperative force of categorization that it does today.

There were just a couple of people who distinguished amphibians as a meaningful category before Darwinian evolution was widely accepted, but the person to put the taxonomic distinctiveness of the Amphibia in the textbooks did so with an evolutionary twist: Ernst Haeckel. Haeckel (1834–1919) was, according to the historian of biology Erik Nordenskiöld (1935), 'the chief source of the world's knowledge of Darwinism', but his methodology and style were distinctive. Whereas English evolution had been built substantially on comparative anatomy and palaeontology, Haeckel added a third type of evidence: embryology. 'The facts of embryology alone would be sufficient to solve the question of man's position in nature', he wrote boldly in his *History of Creation* (1868).[2]

The Swiss physiognomist and clergyman Johann Caspar Lavater created his series 'From Frog to Apollo' to demonstrate human uniqueness, in the light of recent trends to place humans amongst animals. The frog represented the lowliest animal in his version of the chain of being. Coloured etchings by Christian von Mechel after Lavater, 1797.

Haeckel's frogs in his *Kunstformen der Natur* (1904). Haeckel's account of evolution cemented frogs in their status in between water and land animals.

Haeckel's theory of embryos was known as 'recapitulation', or the 'biogenetic law'. In essence, this meant that the evolutionary process that had led upward from primitive organisms to man was echoed in the development of embryos. Embryos passed through primitive states resembling the embryos of their ancestors before reaching the higher form of their species. One phase of the embryological development of man, wrote Haeckel, 'presents us with a change of the fish-like being into a kind of amphibious animal. At a later period the mammal . . . develops out of the amphibian'. Hammering the point home, he went on:

it is in precisely the same succession [as we see in the embryo] that we also see the ancestors of man, and of the higher mammals, appear one after the other in the earth's history; first fishes, then amphibians, later the lower, and at last the higher mammals.[3]

Thus amphibians had a particular place in the embryological evidence for evolution.

What made amphibian embryos important from an evolutionary point of view was, according to Haeckel, their lack of an amnion. The amnion, a membrane that creates a sac surrounding the developing foetus, is present in birds, mammals and the class that we now call reptiles. The fact that frogs' eggs (like fishes') do not possess an amnion put them, for Haeckel, below the others, and made them distinct from their usual classmates the reptiles. Haeckel considered the non-amniotic amphibians as the progenitors of the two branches of amniotic animals: reptiles, subsequently giving rise to birds, and mammals. In the light of this, Haeckel expanded the classes of vertebrates beyond the standard number of four, making the Batrachians (his preferred name for the Amphibia) a class in their own right. Batrachians were the top of the non-amniotes, the closest of their kind to the amniotes in terms of evolutionary development. By the same logic of recapitulation, frogs were at the top of the Batrachians, the very pivotal organism between Haeckel's two fundamental types of vertebrate, amniote and non-amniote. Thus, the cognitive category Amphibia – as opposed to its more inclusive forerunner, reptiles – was constructed with evolution in mind. Before then, it made no sense to separate frogs, toads and newts from lizards, but now that the transition from water to land was scientifically significant, it made sense to consider the animals that embodied the possibility of the change. Haeckel's

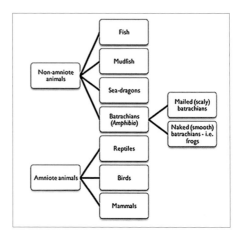

A simplified version of Haeckel's schematic hierarchy of extant vertebrates, 1868. The three columns represent, from L–R, main class, class and subclass. Batrachians occupy the intermediary position between the two main classes.

evolutionary construction of the category spread rapidly, giving impetus to many projects of research.

Haeckel's one-time student Wilhelm Roux (1850–1924) was seduced by the topic of embryos, and his powers of self-promotion have ensured that his achievements now take a prominent place in the history of embryology. Roux was not as interested in the grand evolutionary questions as his mentor, but rather in the immediate causes of embryonic development. How did embryos 'know' what pattern to follow? Were the forces internal, or did they come from the environment? The frog embryo, which was already in experimental use by his colleagues at the University of Breslau, was a good choice for finding out. Unlike mammalian embryos, hidden away in the womb, the frog is fully visible throughout its development.

Edward Pflüger (1829–1910), professor of physiology at Breslau, was one person already using the frog to answer those internal versus external development questions, generally finding that the two interacted to determine how the frog turned

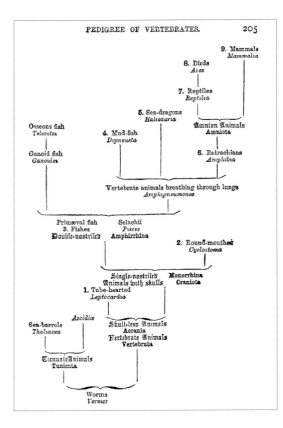

9. Mammals
Mammalia

8. Birds
Aves

7. Reptiles
Reptilia

5. Sea-dragons
Halisauria

Amnion Animals
Amniota

Osseous fish
Teleostei

4. Mud-fish
Dipneusta

Ganoid fish
Ganoidei

6. Batrachians
Amphibia

Vertebrate animals breathing through lungs
Amphipneumones

Primæval fish
3. Fishes
Double-nostrilled

Selachii
Pisces
Amphirrhina

2. Round-mouthed
Cyclostoma

Single-nostrilled
Animals with skulls
1. Tube-hearted
Leptocardia

Monorrhina
Craniota

Sea-barrels
Thaliacea

Ascidiæ

Skull-less Animals
Acrania
Vertebrate Animals
Vertebrata

Tunicate Animals
Tunicata

Worms
Vermes

A phylogenetic (evolutionary history) version of Haeckel's hierarchy, showing batrachians as the ancestors of all land vertebrates, 1868.

out. In one experiment he rotated frogs' eggs on a slowly spinning wheel, and found that the axis along which the egg divided and developed was altered by the absence of a consistent gravitational force.

Roux wondered about a similar set of questions. Did each cell have its own internal developmental drive ('self-differentiation'), or did cells somehow 'talk' to one another ('dependent differentiation')? Roux caricatured Pflüger as a believer in dependent

Half-embryos of a frog, created by Wilhelm Roux, 1890.

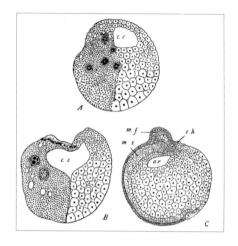

differentiation and set him up as the intellectual straw man that his own experiments would destroy. In the most famous of these, Roux carefully poked a hot needle into one half of a two-cell frog embryo, killing one cell (or 'blastomere'). If development were dependent upon the environment (the position he ascribed to Pflüger), the remaining cell should compensate for its neighbour's loss and produce a normal embryo. If development were independent as Roux claimed, the lone cell should continue regardless to produce a half-embryo.

With great fanfare, Roux reported in 1888 that he had indeed produced a (short-lived) half-tadpole. Roux was right and Pflüger was wrong. This was Roux's story, at any rate. Hans Driesch (1867–1941), another of Haeckel's former pupils then at the Naples Marine Biological Station, tried a similar experiment with sea urchin embryos and got the opposite result: normal, albeit small, embryos. Driesch rather generously explained away the apparent contradiction: development probably *was* internal as Roux claimed, but some regulatory ability was available to compensate when things went wrong. Driesch's experiment had provoked this compensatory mechanism; Roux's would have done too, but he had probably not succeeded in killing the blastomere completely. Driesch's experiment worked because instead of stabbing one cell of the two-cell embryo, he physically shook it apart from its twin.

Roux's disagreement with Driesch highlights an issue that we have already seen in chapter Four, namely what happens when scientists start to downplay the frogness of their experimental subjects and instead treat the frog as a standard organism. Roux was quite explicit about this; he thought that development was a mechanical system and that studying one organism would yield results relevant to all. But as the urchin showed, this was not true, or at least compelled the experimenter to come up with a reason why the test showing the 'wrong' result was invalid.

Most accounts of Roux's fabled experiment fail to convey its practical difficulties. It was actually very hard to carry out; the cells were hard to puncture, and once punctured, the remaining cell was hard to keep alive (only about 20 per cent made it). Most early twentieth-century amphibian experimenters did not consider the basic fact that pure water is toxic to embryos, drawing out their vital salts through osmosis. Moreover, in some of Roux's trials, a normal embryo did develop, and in these instances he was forced to come up with compensating explanations to show that the experiment had gone wrong.

Similar challenges afflicted the embryological work of Hans Spemann (1869–1941) at the University of Würzburg. Spemann was also working at the puzzle of self- versus dependent differentiation, having switched to the frog's close cousin, the salamander, for his experiments. Taking a hair from his baby daughter, with the most dextrous patience he tied it around the embryo of a two-celled salamander embryo. Cloned frogs, or artificial twins, can supposedly be created at home using a technique much the same as Spemann's. The spawn need to be very fresh, as the technique must be done at the two-cell stage. This can be seen, in large-spawned species, against a white background and under a magnifying glass. A hair loop can be used to cut the cells along their join, and the separated cells should now, in theory, develop into two identical tadpoles.

Spemann, however, tightened the noose without proceeding all the way to a cut. He found that by this method he could make the embryo grow into twin, conjoined specimens, and the experiment was repeated with frogs to the same effect. But a slight repositioning of the noose would result in a single larva on one side of the hair, and a blob of meaningless tissue on the other. Why should this be? What made one part of the embryo turn into one thing, and another into something completely different? Spemann turned to the eyes of frog embryos to try to find out, asking what would happen if one moved a bit of embryonic tissue; would it turn into tissue appropriate to the original or the new location?

In a series of experiments, Spemann excised the eye anlages – the cells that would turn into the lens – from frog embryos and transplanted them elsewhere in the embryo. If self-differentiating, they should develop into lenses (so-called 'free lenses') wherever they were transplanted. If dependent in their differentiation, they should not. In 1901, Spemann concluded that the lens did not develop unless it was in contact with the tissue that normally neighboured it. But results coming in from Czech and American biologists claimed that free lenses *were* possible. These results had been obtained using *Rana esculenta* and *R. palustris*, rather than the *R. fusca* used by Spemann, and when Spemann switched to *R. esculenta*, he too obtained free lenses.

These results have become the stuff of scientific myth. With many twists and turns of method and interpretation, Spemann's frogs came to form the basis of today's embryological discipline, developmental biology. But in the process, the frogs have been stripped of their species specificity. How many of today's developmental biologists know that the species described by their hero, '*Rana fusca*', is not even a real species, but rather a local variant of the European common frog, *Rana temporaria*? Just as in Roux's case, it takes work to learn to use a frog, and more work still to strip it of its frogness and transform it into a standard organism that works the same as all other species.

By contrast to Spemann's success story, Haeckel's legacy was to prove tragic for the Austrian zoologist Paul Kammerer (1880–1926), whose attempts to demonstrate developmental evolution in action concluded in a self-administered gunshot to the head. Unlike Roux, and perhaps Spemann, Kammerer cared a great deal about the frogness of his organisms and this know-how,

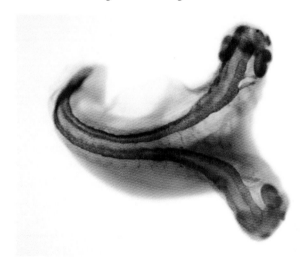

A recent example of an experiment inspired by early amphibian embryology; a tadpole of the western clawed frog, *Xenopus tropicalis*, has been twinned by transplanting a Spemann's organizer from another tadpole into its belly.

Table of normal development of *Rana fusca roesel* (probably *Rana temporaria*) by Friedrich Kopsch, 1952.

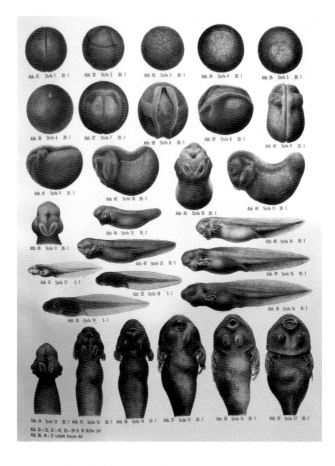

re-cast as lack of objectivity by his enemies, was a partial cause of his downfall. Kammerer was inspired, and ultimately destroyed, by that most tantalizing feature of evolutionary theory; it was, as Chambers had realized, impossible to demonstrate within a human lifespan. (The American T. H. Morgan claimed in the 1920s that his colonies of fruit flies provided such evidence, but many were not convinced and ascribed the flies' mutations merely to their unnatural life within Morgan's lab.) For those raised on the Haeckellian notion of recapitulation, there was a powerful appeal in the evolutionary metaphor of amphibian development; it seemed to say something about the course of evolution. Thus Kammerer set about trying to modify the physical characteristics of Amphibia, and, moreover, to investigate whether such modifications could be inherited by their offspring. In short, he was trying to speed up evolution, using the organism that already seemed to do so.

Kammerer was employed in the old exhibition hall of the Viennese Prater amusement park, recently converted into a state-of-the-art vivarium: a research facility equipped to maintain temperature and humidity exactly as required for its many zoological specimens. During the years before the First World War, Kammerer was able to set up complex, multi-generational experiments at the vivarium, inducing heritable terrestrial characteristics in aquatic salamanders and aquatic characteristics in terrestrial ones. Of all his research, Kammerer was most pleased with his salamander experiments (along with those using the sea squirt *Ciona*), but his most famous – or rather infamous – experiments involved the midwife toad, *Alytes obstetricans*.

Like most frogs and toads, the males of these species sit on top of the female while mating and hold on for several days, but unlike their aquatic cousins they have no need of rough patches (nuptial pads) on their thumbs to stop them slipping off. Kammerer induced his normally terrestrial specimens to breed in the water, then rescued and reared the fertilized eggs that sank to the bottom. By these means, Kammerer claimed to induce the appearance of nuptial pads in the next generation of midwife toads. Astoundingly, these pads appeared to be passed onto *their* offspring.

The midwife toad (*Alytes obstetricans*), subject of Paul Kammerer's ill-fated experiments in evolution.

Although Kammerer's science now seems extraordinary, it had its echoes in both fact and fiction of the time. As historian Sander Gliboff has discovered, Czech experimenters had been working on salamanders as early as 1876, trying to see whether environmental conditions could alter their pigmentation. Other work at the Vienna vivarium concerned the regeneration and transplantation of limbs in salamanders, newts and frogs. The scientific significance of amphibians at this time is further illustrated by the fact that a small clutch of evolutionary, amphibious sci-fi appeared in the 1920s and '30s: Mikhail Bulgakov's *The Fatal Eggs* (1924–6); Alexander Belyaev's *The Amphibian* (1928); Karel Čapek's *War with the Newts* (1936); and the Soviet film *Salamandra* (1928).

Bulgakov – a trained doctor – set his blackly comic frog novel somewhere very like the Vienna vivarium. *The Fatal Eggs* centres upon Professor Persikov, a scientist working at the Zoological

Institute in Moscow who accidentally stumbles upon a red ray which bequeaths enhanced life-powers upon the organisms that it touches. The first organisms to receive these powers are amoebae, and observing their 'furious reproduction' and rapid maturation, Persikov – an amphibian specialist – immediately thinks to try the ray upon frogs. The results are remarkable:

> In the course of two days thousands of tadpoles hatched from the grains of roe. But as if that were not enough, in the course of a single day the tadpoles grew extraordinarily into frogs so vicious and gluttonous that half of them were gobbled up on the spot by the other half. And then those that remained alive began to spawn in no time at all, and in two days, by now without any ray, bred a new generation, and a quite innumerable one at that.[4]

The Mallorcan midwife toad (*Alytes muletensis*) has been a happier research topic for herpetologist Richard Griffiths. The species was thought extinct but was rediscovered in the late 1970s; since then captive breeding has been achieved and understanding of its ecological requirements greatly improved.

But before he can experiment any further, Persikov's equipment is requisitioned by the State. The country's chickens have all died in a mysterious plague, and the authorities want to replace them by breeding up superior stock from imported German eggs. Unfortunately, however, the hens' eggs have been accidentally replaced by snakes' eggs, and under the influence of the ray these emerge as monstrous, people-eating prodigies.

The story is in large part political satire, a tale of humans fatally transformed by the red ray of Marxist-Leninism. The batrachian nature of the people, involuntary subjects of political experiment, is evidenced by their frequently 'croaking' voices, especially on the telephone. Urban crowds pullulate like frogspawn; the military and civilian masses are snake-like forces that eventually crush Persikov and his assistants in just the manner that the constricting serpents kill their first victims. On a simpler level, however, frogs were for Bulgakov – just as they were for Kammerer – the natural experimental organism of evolution.

In August 1926, after years of doubt over Kammerer's results, the American herpetologist G. K. Noble travelled to Vienna to observe the sole surviving specimen of midwife toad. He returned to New York, and reported bluntly in the journal *Nature* that the pads had been faked; black ink had been injected under the skin to produce them. One month later, Kammerer shot himself. Most commentators have taken Kammerer's suicide as an admission of guilt, but his sympathetic biographer Arthur Koestler gives alternative explanations, ranging from his difficult private life to confusion and embarrassment over the fraud; Koestler suggests that the ink injection might even have been perpetrated without Kammerer's knowledge by anti-communist saboteurs.

Kammerer's reputation as a 'wizard with lizards' counted at least as much against him as it did for him, for it made it very difficult for others to replicate his results, or even feel inclined to try. Even picking the eggs out of the water and rearing them to adulthood was a painstaking task. Kammerer's experiments also lasted many years. The whole point was to see whether altered characteristics were heritable, requiring generations of breeding to find out. (Moreover, the nuptial pads were only present during the breeding season, so killing a precious specimen to preserve evidence – as his critics demanded – meant one less for breeding.) Part of the criticism of Kammerer can therefore be ascribed to an emerging split between biology and natural history: between those who prescribed a lengthy engagement with the animal in its own right, and those who believed they knew animals through more general laboratory or statistical methods.

Commentary on the midwife toad episode peaked in the mid-twentieth century, and writers were more or less unanimous in painting Kammerer's guiding theory as a fundamentally silly one (hence necessitating fraud for its demonstration). The word most often used for Kammerer's work is 'Lamarckian', by which commentators have meant an anti-Darwinian biology of acquired inheritance – antelopes that purposefully evolve into giraffes by stretching their necks ever higher for leaves. In fact, central and Eastern European biologists such as Kammerer and his boss Hans Przibram counted themselves firmly as Darwinians.[5] However, their Darwinism was refracted through the lens of Haeckel. Bulgakov's description of the ray-zapped tadpoles reveals just such a hybrid understanding of evolution: there is competition among members of the same species ('half of them were gobbled up . . . by the other half'), but also changed bodily features that persist in the organisms' inheritance ('without any ray [they] bred a new generation'). This Haeckellian version of evolution was a mis-match with the Anglo-American tradition.

Kammerer was, in fact, sympathetic to the critical suggestion that his experiments might not demonstrate forward evolution. It was quite possible that instead he was inducing regression: stimulating the display of ancestral characteristics that were no longer necessary for the species in normal life. He was in good company, as Gliboff has found; some German biologists of the 1920s suggested that creatures could regress to a primitive form, endowed with more potency and flexibility than their usual, highly evolved variety. It was even possible that this bodily plasticity was itself a heritable characteristic: that a creature which had regressed to its more potent form made it easier for its offspring to do the same. Hence the research at the vivarium regarding amphibians' regeneration of missing limbs. In this context, Kammerer's work does not look like an attempt to fast-forward Lamarckian evolution as his critics have claimed, but rather to demonstrate the recapitulatory framework of Haeckellian evolution.

Such youthful flexibility in the adult amphibian suggested something biologically special, and indeed in the 1920s a theory about it was developed. It was called paedomorphosis, and was announced by its proposer as a 're-statement' of Haeckel's bio-genetic law. Paedomorphosis described a phenomenon whereby adult creatures displayed features normally associated with the juvenile of the species. The phenomenon was most dramatically displayed by animals whose juvenile and adult characteristics were normally separated by a Rubicon of complete metamorphosis; once again, amphibians were in the scientific limelight. Nature contains several species of Amphibia that look like over-sized tadpoles but can nevertheless breed, of which the best known is probably the axolotl. Having identified the thyroid gland as the thing that controlled metamorphosis, in 1919 scientists experimented to see if frogs too could be induced to breed in their tadpole state. By removing the thyroid anlage in embryos of the wood frog, *Rana sylvatica*, they obtained giant larvae, two to three times normal size. The tadpoles never matured, but scientists could not get them to breed in their larval form.

In his retirement, Spemann made his most 'fantastical' suggestion yet: that an entire frog might be generated by implanting the early embryo nucleus from one egg into another, unfertilized one. Would the organizer principle be able to work on an egg that was not primed for development? In 1952, American researchers Robert Briggs and Thomas King managed just this feat using the high school lab favourite, the northern leopard frog, *Rana pipiens*, raising tadpoles from unfertilized eggs that had had an embryonic nucleus inserted. Briggs and King found that the earlier the developmental stage of the donor embryo, the greater the chance of success – the development of an apparently normal tadpole. Nuclei removed from embryos that had matured so far as to develop a nervous system were not successful at all. At Oxford in the late 1950s and early 1960s, John Gurdon (1933–) attempted to replicate the feat with later-stage nuclei. Gurdon used a different species of frog – *Xenopus laevis* – and inserted nuclei from fully developed tadpole cells into eggs with their nuclei removed. Gurdon's eggs went on to develop, each one producing a larva genetically identical to its donor. However, they died without metamorphosing into adult frogs, just like all attempts ever since – and no one knows why.

If I were a member of *Xenopus laevis* rather than *Homo sapiens*, I might point to Gurdon's period as the great era in which my species commenced its colonization of the globe. There were just a few breeding colonies of these creatures in Europe at the beginning of the twentieth century, but by its end the species had become the experimental organism par excellence for developmental biologists around the world, and had even been sent into space.[6] *X. laevis* was popularized by Lancelot Hogben (1895–1975), the British socialist who, having moved to South Africa, found it such a 'godsend' for research that he named his house after it, and brought a colony of the species back with him when he returned to the UK in 1930. Hogben's research continued the hormonal strand of frog biology that had begun with the thyroid induction or suppression of metamorphosis, and in London his team began using *X. laevis* to try and develop a human pregnancy test. At that time, the only method involved injecting rodents with the urine of possibly pregnant women, then killing the mouse or rabbit to see the state of their ovaries.

The frogs, however, were such sensitive registers of human chorionic gonadotropin (a hormone produced by pregnant women) that it was not necessary to kill them to confirm the result. Instead, they themselves would ovulate only eight to twelve hours after a positive injection, laying their eggs for all to see. For the next 30 years, hospitals around the world kept

The African clawed frog (*Xenopus laevis*), favoured subject for hormonal and developmental laboratory investigation.

Xenopus laevis was the most reliable test for pregnancy in the 1940s and '50s.

colonies of *X. laevis* in their basements, ready to confirm doubtful pregnancies. Excess specimens were sometimes released into the wild, and occasionally they escaped, forming feral colonies. Ironically, it was very difficult to breed the frogs in captivity, but gradually their keepers discovered how they could take advantage of the hormonal injections to produce actual breeding – as opposed to just egg-laying – at will.

Once it possessed the convenient quality of breeding on demand, *Xenopus* rapidly became a favoured animal for all sorts of research. Using frogs elicited few pangs of conscience, and now this tough species could be easily procured without resorting to Helmholtz's annual frog-hunting frenzy. But *X. laevis* also has properties that ought to count against its use;

slow to mature, it has an anomalous pattern of development and a complex genetics, with four copies of each gene rather than the usual two. Tradition is, however, its own justification, for learning to breed and keep a reliable colony of usable animals requires a considerable investment of time and skill. Once scientists have learned how to breed and look after a species, it makes sense to stick with it. When it comes to molecular biology and genetics, it is absolutely essential that everyone is talking about the same species. A 'model organism' needs to be like a standardized instrument that everyone understands and knows how to calibrate. Hence scientists have by and large stuck with *X. laevis*. By about 1990, publications on *X. laevis* in developmental biology outnumbered those on other amphibians by a factor of approximately 50 to one, although these days its cousin *X. tropicalis* (which possesses the standard dual-copy of genes) is increasingly used for genetic research. *X. laevis* remains a favourite for molecular biology; scientists are using it today to find ways of replacing damaged tissue – such as heart, brain or blood cells – in humans.

The fantasy of regenerating humans by recourse to the frog's body is one that the 1920s sci-fi writers would have recognized instantly. Just like theirs, it keys into a popular discourse of evolution: of taking the species on to the next level, or of the natural flexibility and potency contained within the metamorphosing body. As such, it has something in common with Haeckel's biogenetic law. Central to the conceptualization of amphibians, this 'law' retained a remarkably persistent intuitive appeal long after all its specific claims had been overridden. A sex education manual of 1917 asserted: 'Every frog which reaches maturity repeats again the story of his race in his earlier stages.'[7] Even in 1977, the biologist Stephen Jay Gould claimed that most of his colleagues still secretly thought there was 'something to it'.[8]

When Richard Wassersug began his long career in frog studies around the same time, he found that Haeckellian perspectives were still shaping batrachian classification. There were, he recalls, 'two conflicting phylogenies [evolutionary family trees] . . . one based on adult anurans and the other on tadpoles'. To find out which of these was right, Wassersug began looking in detail at tadpoles. His work focused on their complex mouthparts, and caused him to realize that frogs were extremely specialized and well-adapted to life in their larval form. They were not, as adult-based phylogenies implied, merely '"fish" or imperfect frogs'. Such phylogenies were implicitly Haeckellian in form, while Wassersug's work was, in his own words, 'a non Haeckellian line of inquiry'.[9]

Haeckel is rather like the disreputable uncle at the family party of developmental biologists, and recapitulation is today a dirty word in science. Whether scientists like it or not, Haeckel's frogs have inspired many branches of developmental science through the nineteenth and twentieth centuries. Thanks to Haeckel's way of seeing things, the frog's emergence from water to land has become emblematic of a whole chapter in the evolution of life. Its embodiment of life's power, waiting to unfold, has placed it at the heart of both successful and unsuccessful science. The frog has been a vivacious embryo, a chemically sensitive collection of developing cells: even, perhaps, a source of human regeneration.

6 Of Frogs and Fruitfulness

Swarming and flickering in a shallow pond, tadpoles are a most vivid symbol of nature's irrepressible urge to reproduce. Frogs can appear in vast numbers overnight, a phenomenon of synchronized reproduction that is known by biologists as 'explosive breeding'. If a frog laid its eggs on its own, the whole lot might be eaten by a predator. But if every frog oviposits at once there is a good chance that, although many eggs will be eaten, *some* eggs from any given individual frog will survive: hence its selective advantage. The Ancient Egyptian tadpole hieroglyphic commemorated this astonishing fecundity of the frog, standing for the otherwise unthinkably large number of 100,000.

The appearance of the frogs that produce and fertilize all these eggs can be no less astonishing. All sorts of strange explanations have been advanced for the sudden mass appearance of frogs in nature. A Victorian traveller to Panama reported:

> Toads and other frog-like animals are most numerous during the wet season . . . So prodigious is their number after rain, that the popular prejudice is that the drops of rain are changed into toads; and even the more learned maintain, that the eggs of this animal are raised with the vapour from the adjoining swamps, and being conveyed to the city by the rains, are there hatched . . . After a night

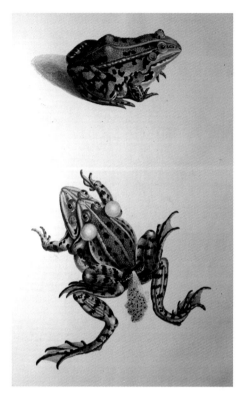

Frogs mating (either the pool frog, *Pelophylax lessonae*, or the marsh frog, *Pelophylax ridibundus*), illustrated in Roesel von Rosenhof's *Historia Naturalis Ranarum Nostratium* (1758).

of rain, the streets are almost covered with them, and it is impossible to walk without crushing some.[1]

Frogs emerge thus *en masse* in order to mate. George Orwell found the sight a deeply appealing one, ascribing to the male (perhaps wistfully?) a 'phase of intense sexiness'. Orwell found that 'if you offer him . . . your finger, he will cling to it with surprising strength and take a long time to discover that it is not a female toad'.[2] This triumph of urge over precision has frequent unfortunate results. Females may drown in the iron grip of their mates, and even passing fish may be harmed or killed if they fall into the male's clutches. The sight of a pond heaving with randy frogs, rolling about in couples, threesomes and even foursomes, has given the Anura a powerful life with human fertility and sex.

Recently, in European culture at least, the emphasis seems to be on the mass mating rather than the spawning: the sex, not the fertility. The most striking recent example treats the anurans as did Orwell: as pure sex, rather than reproduction. It occurs in Patrick Süskind's 1985 novel *Perfume*, whose anti-hero is the strikingly named Grenouille (frog). Grenouille murders women for their scent, and on the day that he is due to be executed for his crimes, the scent of the women – including that of his intended final victim – overpowers the crowd and changes the scene from one of public execution to a giant batrachian orgy.

The massed mating of frogs in spring-time has made them a symbol of unrestrained sexuality for many observers.

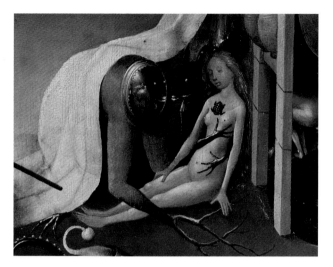

This unsettling detail from Bosch's *Garden of Earthly Delights* (1490–1510) places batrachian sexuality in a decidedly negative theological light.

There is also a limited amount of evidence connecting earlier European culture with anurans as agents of fecundity,[3] although such links may originate in the characteristic swelling-up of frogs and toads – reminiscent of the fruitful womb – rather than their breeding behaviour. The sixteenth-century philosopher and physician Paracelsus called frogspawn 'the sperm of the world'. The links with fertility are there in a negative sense too; if used correctly, frogs can actually prevent it. In England, a woman that places a frog in her mouth and spits three times will not conceive that year.[4] In the 1950s, the deputy of China's National People's Congress famously exhorted women to swallow live tadpoles as a means to restrict their fertility; when an experiment was carried out to test the efficacy of this traditional peasant contraceptive, it performed disastrously and the advice was retracted.[5]

In lands that are reliant on periodic flooding for agriculture, the appearance of frogs coincides with that of the water that

Ancient Egyptian depiction of Seti I (reg. *c.* 1294–1279 BCE) making an offering to the frog goddess Heket.

brings life to the crops; the frogspawn is a sign that the people too will eat and reproduce for another year. No wonder, then, that in Ancient Egypt – dependent upon the flooding Nile for its agriculture – the goddess of fertility and birth took the form of a frog. Her name was Heket; midwives were her servants, and women often kept amulets in her shape to protect them during childbirth. (In a somewhat similar vein, Pliny the Elder later recommended that a stick which had been used to get a frog out of a snake would speed up labour; unfortunately, he neglected to mention where such a stick might be found or precisely how it should be deployed.) Statuettes of Heket exist from as far back as *c.* 3000 BCE; she appears in a papyrus myth of the Middle Kingdom (*c.* 1600 BCE) and there is evidence of cults in her honour in both Middle and Upper Egypt. Although she was most often pictured as a frog-headed woman, Heket was also portrayed as a whole frog, or even as a frog atop a phallus. This last image makes clear Heket's connection not just with birth but also with fertility, a connection that was reinforced by the cults

Although many Ancient Egyptian women kept Heket frog amulets to bring them luck in childbirth, this travertine example (2950–2770 BCE) is thought to have been kept in a temple due to its relatively large size (approximately 15cm in each dimension).

that considered her to be a consort of Khnum. Khnum was god of the Nile's source, and moulder of children's bodies from the silty clay that washed in each year with the floods. Together, the floodwater and its frogs brought humans to birth.

Dating from a similar period to the Heket papyrus, the Manduka Sukta (frog hymn) of the Hindu Rigveda praises the life-giving monsoon in batrachian form:

Green and Spotty have vouchsafed us treasure.
The Frogs who give us cows in hundreds lengthen our
    lives in this most fertilizing season.

The words of Brahmans, who have waited until the appointed time to fulfil their religious vows, are rather sweetly compared to the sound of the frogs greeting the rain – for which they have

also patiently waited. A few hundred years later, Europeans, too, caught onto the connection between frogs and rain. European tree frogs (then classified *Rana arborea*, now *Hyla arborea*) reliably strike up their chorus before rainfall, causing them to be dubbed 'living barometers'.[6] In April 1789, the British *New Lady's Magazine* described a more convenient device 'lately discovered at Paris' (although probably originating in Germany): a bottle with water and earth in the bottom; a ladder ascending from them; and a tree frog. The frog would perch at the top of the ladder as long as fair weather could be expected to last, but would return to the water when rain was due. Any English lady attempting to build this herself would have struggled, since *Rana arborea* is not native to Britain and the instruction to 'take one of those small green frogs which are found in hedges' would have resulted in a long, long search.

Many Native American peoples enshrine in their traditional tales the role of the frog in bringing rain and fertility. Several tribes share versions of a myth about a giant monster, Aglebamu, who swallowed the water source of the people. In some versions, he is like a giant frog, and in others he is turned into a frog by the hero Glooskap. Either way, he is made to release the water that the people need.

A Navajo tale tells a different story about how Frog brought water to the people. After Coyote stole fire, it is said, he accidentally set the mountain alight, and First Woman could not get water from the spring, the river or the lake to put it out. The last place she could think to try was the swamp. Frog agreed to help and soaked up a tremendous quantity of water in his porous coat; Crane carried him over the mountain where he squeezed it all back out and extinguished the fire. Frog and Crane made the woman promise to take no more water from their swamp, for it was now nearly dry. The mist that rose up from the water on the

This frog (likely *Hyla arborea*) climbs a glass vessel in Roesel von Rosenhof's *Historia Naturalis Ranarum Nostratium* (1758), reminiscent of the frog barometers popular in late 18th-century Europe.

Many Native American groups revere frogs for their connection with life-giving water. This woollen shaman's tunic, decorated with frogs, is from the Gitskan people (one of whose four clans is Frog).

A golden frog pendant of unknown symbolism, from the Coclé culture (modern-day Panama), 600–800 CE.

mountain became clouds full of rain, and the tale thus teaches that the frog brings the rain. When you hear the frog calling, the story explains, you should try and catch him and tie him up in the cornfield, so that he will bring rain to the crops.[7] In a similar vein, the Zuni tribe of New Mexico traditionally create fertility fetishes in the form of frogs and bury them near water sources, in order to ensure their continued production.

Modern Europeans, no less than Egyptians and Native Americans, have turned to the frog in order to understand fertility and generation. There is a strong and pervasive cultural memory in Britain and the US that sex education in the mid-twentieth century was somehow conveyed – albeit euphemistically and unsuccessfully – through the use of frogs. Carol Ann Duffy's poem 'In Mrs Tilscher's Class' (1990) captures the child's unspeakable puzzlement at nature and its sexual mysteries, all embodied within the classroom frog:

> Over the Easter term the inky tadpoles changed
> from commas into exclamation marks . . .
> . . . A rough boy
> told you how you were born. You kicked him, but stared
>   at your parents, appalled, when you got back home.
> . . . You asked her
> how you were born and Mrs Tilscher smiled,
> then turned away . . .

'Our teacher was . . . clearly embarrassed', recalls one former pupil in a BBC web article. 'We . . . never progressed, in five years, beyond the lifecycle of a frog.' When one of her class fell pregnant, the teacher made a remark that revealed her somewhat unrealistic pedagogical expectations: 'I can't understand it, she attended my classes.' Obviously children were supposed to make the connections for themselves, but as the blogged recollections of a former Catholic schoolgirl make clear, these were not always biologically sound:

> It started in grade four with the ancient movies that showed a female frog leaving her eggs in the stream to be fertilized by the male frog at a later time. So needless to say I thought that babies . . . happened in your sleep (or a stream) until I was at least in grade seven.

The visual similarity between tadpoles and sperm viewed under the microscope (remarked upon at least as far back as 1678) has perhaps served to strengthen the uneasy conviction that the frogs are somehow supposed to be our teachers when it comes to the facts of life. However, the specific source of the remembered connection between frogs and sexual education is probably two-fold. Dissecting frogs has long been a ubiquitous feature of classroom biology, and the sexual organs noted as a part of this process; in their feverish state of not-knowing, children have tried to connect up what they see in the frog with what they want to find out about humans. Secondly, as Duffy's poem describes, tadpoles have commonly been kept in the class and observed as they metamorphose into frogs through the summer term. In this guise, they illustrate a 'cycle of life' which, as historian Julian Carter argues, was central to sex education during the inter-war years.[8]

In this pedagogical model, which still resonates today, teachers treated the bigger pattern of nature's replenishment and avoided a focus upon the sexual act itself. The frog was a perfect choice for this teaching method. With its metamorphic life cycle it made a beautiful point about life's grand story, and with its external method of fertilization it avoided certain embarrassing features of human reproduction. Frogs took their place in a hierarchy of animal forms – the 'ladder of back-boned animals' – that was used to teach about sex. The reproductive differences between these levels of animal were not defined, as one might expect, in the mechanics of congress of egg and sperm, but rather in the quality of parenting. 'The Mother Fish Neglects Her Babies', explained one American pamphlet, placing her firmly at the bottom of the hierarchy that peaked with caring human mothers. Batrachians were little better, at least according to the narrator of a British sex education film of 1932. 'Reptiles [sic] are . . . careless parents', he intoned. 'The frog abandons her eggs . . . and the tadpoles developing within never know the meaning of a mother's care.'[9] However, according to most, frogs took their place in the explanatory framework somewhere between feckless fish and loving mammals. Unlike the former, they at least bequeathed their eggs some protective jelly before swimming off.

The British sex educator Cyril Bibby (1914–1987) was not one to wrap up the facts of life in euphemisms of parenthood, but even he made special pedagogical use of the frog in the animal stories that he wrote for the *New Pioneer* magazine in the late 1930s. With the possible exception of the earthworms, Freda and Freddie are the most explicit of Bibby's alliterative protagonists:

The male frog lies on top of the female, grasping her under the armpits with his thumbs. Mrs Frog gives out into the water her eggs and Mr Frog emits the male cells, or sperm. Each egg joins with a sperm, and that is the start of a new frog . . . Freddie had little pads on his thumbs which Freda did not have, and he used these in holding tightly to her while they were mating . . .[10]

Freddie and Freda are close enough to humans for the sexual comparison to be made, but far enough away to remain decent.

It is not just sex educators, but also sex researchers who have made extensive use of frogs. Besides being extremely numerous in nature, frogs' eggs are noteworthy for their large size and easy visibility, and this was a convenient feature for the early modern philosophers who attempted to unravel the mysteries of reproduction. There were many controversies in the modern period concerning the role of eggs and male fluid in the generation of life, and the priest and natural philosopher Lazzaro Spallanzani (1729–1799) was prominent among those using the frog to explore them.[11] Spallanzani was disinclined to trust the work of one Professor Menzius, who supposed that the male frog's seed was emitted from his toe, and somehow penetrated through the female's thorax to effect fertilization. Another piece of doubtful research came from a Monsieur Gautier, who claimed

Lazzaro Spallanzani's research on the sex life of frogs (among other topics) is celebrated in this statue of 1888 in his birthplace, Scandiano.

that the frog foetus actually came from the male: little mini-tadpoles that 'fed' upon the female egg and grew. Spallanzani was dismissive of this 'pretended discovery' for various reasons, not least that he found Gautier's 'worms' in the female frog's bladder as well as the male.[12] However, Spallanzani *was* persuaded by the experiments of Jan Swammerdam that frogs' eggs were fertilized by the male outside the female's body. Carefully observing and dissecting fertilized and unfertilized eggs, Spallanzani found that the two were absolutely identical. In 1767, Spallanzani concluded that the tadpole existed in the egg before fertilization, wanting only the 'fecundating liquid of the male to unfold [itself]'.[13] On the basis of this discovery, Spallanzani proceeded to promote frogs up the great chain of nature, considering them to be viviparous, like mammals, rather than oviparous like the lower creatures.

The discovery of the tadpole-within-the-egg provoked a cascade of further questions in Spallanzani's mind, and over the following decade he was able to devise experiments to go where his thoughts led him. Borrowing the idea of one of his correspondents, Spallanzani constructed some little trousers of waxed taffeta which he proceeded to fit on his male frogs; thus clad in a sort of whole-body prophylactic, the frogs did not succeed in fathering tadpoles by the females that they mounted. Unlike his correspondent, Spallanzani succeeded in finding droplets of the males' wasted liquor inside their waterproof breeches. He scraped it up and dabbed it on ripe eggs harvested from inside a female, and thus, in 1777, the first artificial fertilization of any animal was achieved. Vanquishing Gautier's crazy ideas once and for all (or so he hoped), Spallanzani found this worked both with and without the worms in the seminal fluid. He also thought that electricity might work instead of seminal fluid in stimulating the development of the egg, but found that it did

Scenes such as this (illustrated here in Roesel von Rosenhof's *Historia Naturalis Ranarum Nostratium*) caused Spallanzani to conclude that 'nothing can be more salacious than the male toad'.

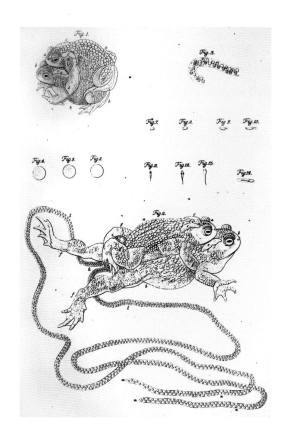

not. Nor did other bodily fluids from the frog, or seminal fluids from other species.

Spallanzani also found himself drawing conclusions about the sexual behaviour of batrachians. Noting that several naturalists believed frogs and toads embraced one another for a biblical period of forty days, he found that the period was actually shorter than this, although still measured in days rather than hours. Observing the toad's fierce embrace, lasting beyond the

154

female's emission of eggs and resisting removal at all costs, Spallanzani judged that 'nothing can be more salacious than the male [toad]'.[14] (However, he qualified this by advising that the toad might be put off his 'nuptials' if too obviously observed by the experimenter.) 'Brutes are not exempt from jealousy', Spallanzani ruminated; perhaps the toad was worried that if he quit too soon, another might get in on the act.

Spallanzani's sexual toad, fecund and grasping, is remarkably similar to the Chinese frog Ch'an Chu, a prosperity symbol and traditional bringer of luck. Perhaps the similarity is not so surprising, for wealth and procreation are universally and tightly linked in human culture. The happy ending always brings fortune, marriage and the birth of children, all of which can be symbolized by the frog. Figurines of Ch'an Chu depict him squatting possessively atop his pile of old coins. More money is threaded on the strings emerging from his mouth and draped over his three-legged body, while his malevolent red eyes dare you to steal the coin that he holds in his open mouth. In terms of cultural significance, Ch'an Chu is currently most significant within the globalized phenomenon of Feng Shui and its internet sales. Supposedly essential in any home or business that wants to thrive, he should be placed in the living room of a home or the main room of a business, diagonally opposite the main entrance. Sometimes the toad (or frog – the term is used interchangeably for Ch'an Chu) has the Buddha on his back for good measure.

There is some doubt as to whether the powers of Ch'an Chu lie in attracting new money or merely in protecting what you already have. Most of the many Feng Shui websites which will sell you a statuette err on the side of optimism and claim that it will do both. Feng Shui expert, Lillian Too, suggests that purchasing up to nine frogs from her online store (at $49.99 each, a total of almost $450) will 'invite more wealth to the house'.

An example of the 'traditional' lucky Feng Shui toad, Ch'an Chu.

Participants in Feng Shui web forums have unfortunately found some of Too's instructions ambiguous, and there is considerable debate about, for example, the direction in which the frogs should face for failsafe financial gain. On balance, it would seem safe to say that the best way to obtain money from lucky frogs is by selling them.

There are so many frog myths in southern China that it is extremely difficult to disentangle the origins of this contemporary good luck charm. It seems to be based on at least two stories, but has deeper roots still in a multitude of southern Chinese batrachian myths and customs. Frogs have traditionally been eaten, deified and sacrificed in southern China. In Guangdong and Jiangxi, wa frog cults were widespread and included versions of the frog king tale. One magical frog helped to repair a burst dyke in 1115 CE and was rewarded with a temple; frogs were also sacrificed or put into earth altars as part of a rain ceremony. (The custom persisted in the form of placing three-legged toad figures in old latrines.)

On the more sinister side, the dark aspect of the human soul was depicted as a ha-ma frog. A tradition from the Thai border of southern China also has a negative connotation for batrachians, ranking the toad as one of five venomous creatures. However, this property can be turned to positive use by placing the animal (or a representation of it) in key locations on the fifth day of the fifth month, thus driving out disease and evil. A frog broth may also be consumed around this time, and drawing on the ground with a dried toad's foot will cause water to start flowing there.[15]

One obvious source story for the Feng Shui frog concerns an envious wife who stole the elixir of immortality and fled with it to the Moon. Here, she was transformed into a toad with three legs – just like Ch'an Chu – representing three phases of the moon.[16] The three-legged toad in the Moon dates back at least to the poet Li Bai (701–762 CE), and the outline of a toad can still, it is claimed, be seen there at night. A tradition of eating frogs in the fifth month appears to connect this lunar frog with a role in fertility. Held at Full Moon during the mating period of the frogs, this festival of frog-eating celebrates the sexual congress of Heaven and Earth.

A second well-known Chinese frog story concerns the immortal holy man Liu Hai, and in its different versions his toad Ch'an Chu takes on different qualities. According to some, the toad is his consort and helps him travel instantaneously to new locations. However, the toad also has a propensity to sulk and hide down wells and from time to time Liu Hai must lure him out with a string of coins. In other versions, the toad in the well is actually evil, emanating lethal vapours, and is tempted out with the coins so that he can be killed by Liu Hai. In still another account, Liu Hai's toad turns into a girl and marries him.

A 20th-century woodcut of the immortal Liu Hai sporting with his three-legged toad.

Thus the three legs of the Feng Shui frog connect it with the Moon, with protection from disease and perhaps with enhanced fertility. The string of coins connects it with Liu Hai (who, incidentally, is a Taoist figure, making the Buddha on Ch'an Chu's back an incongruous addition). Whichever version of the Liu Hai story we take, the toad's avarice is not a particularly admirable quality – even the means of his undoing – and the use of the toad for luck is not an easy fit with the logic of Western iconography. At least one Chinese specialist gives a similarly negative account of the motif, stating that the toad in the Moon symbolizes the unattainable while Liu Hai's toad represents how money can lure men to their destruction.[17] Nor, it would seem, is the tradition of using Ch'an Chu's statuette for luck so ancient as sellers of Feng Shui accoutrements routinely claim. Three-legged toad figurines pre-date the Liu Hai story by many hundreds of years, and during the Han dynasty were often carved in jade,[18] but figurines of 'Liu Hai sporting with the toad' do not seem to emerge in significant numbers until the eighteenth century. Such figures, which were indeed considered auspicious, became more common in the nineteenth century. However, the form in which they are now sold is shorn of Liu Hai. This is a very recent phenomenon; I can find no evidence of the present-day format, showing Ch'an Chu alone, before the late twentieth century. It would appear to be a significant change from the logic of luck which required both Liu Hai and his toad to be present in earlier carvings. It is almost as though the tale of Liu Hai is too distracting or irrelevant for contemporary Feng Shui purchasers, many of whom are not of Chinese background. And yet, it is not quite that simple, for the tale of Liu Hai (or a short, bastardized version thereof) is generally presented on Feng Shui websites to add authenticity to the object. Despite its problematic iconology and doubtful authenticity, the lucky money frog has now taken its place in the marketplace of consumable 'spirituality', a result of the general fondness of Westerners for frogs and the allure of Chinese exoticism, combined with the frog's ancient association with fruitfulness of all kinds.

7 Jumped Up

Be kind and tender to the Frog,
And do not call him names,
As 'Slimy skin,' or 'Polly-wog,'
Or likewise 'Ugly James,'
Or 'Gape-a-grin,' or 'Toad-gone-wrong,'
Or 'Billy Bandy-knees':
The Frog is justly sensitive
To epithets like these.

Hilaire Belloc's 1896 poem 'The Frog' works by cutting slyly across its own admonition. Despite advising against the calling of names, it then goes on to give an unnecessarily long list of suggestions. It seems as though the poet has ceased giving examples after 'Ugly James', but he unexpectedly continues, with just a bit too much enthusiasm and inventiveness. At the poem's end, Belloc concedes with pretended reluctance that those who stick up for frogs are 'extremely rare'. The verse is, contrary to its stated intent, an invitation to laugh at batrachians. Even herpetologists, those professional students of the frog, have been forced to confront the unscientific but seemingly unavoidable question: why are frogs so funny? In a serious research paper, three of them conclude that frogs' short, squat bodies, their 'surprising saltatory gait' and their harmlessness are the source of

humour. One might plausibly add bug-eyes and explosive croaks to this list, and even theorize that recent frog humour is in part a guilty normalization of anurans' role in scientific experiment. However, one can only agree with the authors' conclusion that collectively, these characteristics render them 'both bizarre and benign': beasts of 'intrinsic whimsy'.[1] Some species even have an upwardly curving mouth that makes them look as though they are sharing the joke.

The comedy value of frogs dates back to at least the sixth century BCE, when Aesop told unflattering fables at their expense. The proud frog, attempting to imitate the mighty ox, inflates itself until it bursts. The frogs that persistently importune Zeus for a king are eventually rewarded with a crane that eats them up. In another piece of frog humour from the ancient world, the *Batrachomyomachia* savours the ridiculousness of the frogs. This, the first known comic epic (c. fifth century BCE), tells a tale of deadly revenge and war . . . of frogs and mice. The frog king starts the whole thing off by giving a mouse a lift across the river

This illustration of 'The Battle of Frogs and Mice' was made for John Ogilby's *Fables of Aesop* (1665). The tale is not usually attributed to Aesop.

and carelessly allowing him to drown *en route*. When the mice rise up in armed response, the gods refuse to intervene. Instead, they sit back and enjoy the altercation, finding it doubly funny because the two equally insignificant parties take it so seriously.

The humour of the *Batrachomyomachia* is in some ways not so very far from Mark Twain's story, 'The Celebrated Jumping Frog of Calaveras County' (1865). A large part of Twain's comedy lies in the *mise en scène*: the narrator has been set up by his friend to suffer the interminable anecdotes of Simon Wheeler, propping up the bar in the dilapidated Angels hotel. Wheeler himself is suspiciously batrachian; fat and bald, he tells his stories with a comic earnestness: 'Far from his imagining that there was

anything ridiculous or funny about his story, he regarded it as a really important matter.' Wheeler's tale (when he gets round to it) concerns an inveterate gambler, Smiley, who catches and trains a frog to be a magnificent jumper. 'Smiley said all a frog wanted was education, and he could do 'most anything', reports Wheeler. When a stranger comes into town, Smiley bets him that his frog can out-jump any other. The stranger agrees to the bet, but while Smiley is off catching a frog for his adversary, he sneakily fills Smiley's prize jumper with leaden quail shot. When the race begins, Smiley's frog remains 'planted as solid as a church', and after the stranger has hot-footed it with his $40, Smiley continues to scratch his head. 'I wonder if there ain't something the matter with him', he ponders of his frog. 'He 'pears to look mighty baggy, somehow.'

Some time later, Twain came upon a translation of the tale into French, and took it upon himself to translate it back into English, aiming to show the 'odious . . . bad grammar' that the French version had imposed upon his story. The translation is nowhere near as bad as Twain makes out in his humorous attempt to 'claw' it back to 'civilized language'. For example, he is either ignorant, or pretends to be ignorant, of such basic French constructions as the 'ne . . . pas' double form of negative. Twain doggedly mistranslates each instance to highlight what he regards as nothing more than grammatical recalcitrance on the part of the French: 'Eh bien! I no saw not that that frog had nothing of better than each frog.' American readers of the mid- to late nineteenth century were used to the connection of frogs and the French, and so this linguistic parody – the frog's own version – adds another dimension to Twain's original story.

However, a little prying into US journals of the nineteenth century suggests that when Americans heard of the French as frogs or frog-eaters, it was usually in the context of the English.

In this Japanese frog battle, the anurans' opponents are snakes. Woodblock print by Utagawa Yoshitsuya (1822–66).

A competitor urges his frog on at the annual re-creation of Twain's contest in Calaveras County.

Either it was an English author making the connection (notably Charles Dickens, who was widely read in the US), or else the slur was made by an English character. With this in mind, a seemingly trivial part of Twain's tale attains fresh significance. Part of Wheeler's lead-up to the frog story concerns Smiley's dog, also the object of his owner's bets. This dog is a bulldog, and its *modus operandi* in fights is to take firm hold of its opponent's hind leg until the latter gives up. The bulldog is eventually beaten by a trickster who enters a two-legged canine into the ring (the back legs have been lost in an accident with a circular saw). Not knowing where to bite, Smiley's dog gives up, loses the fight and dies of shame. The dog is a bulldog – the variety most closely associated with the English. Its inescapably English nature is highlighted by Twain, who claims that the French translator, not knowing what it would even be in his own language, renders it as 'bouledogue'. Thus in the palimpsest version of the

166

tale, English-French-English, both the English bulldog and the French frog are bested by American wit.

Twain's story continues to celebrate American identity in its eponymous county, and is annually re-enacted (without the lead shot, which would be poisonous to the frogs). The contest started in 1928 and, notwithstanding a rift and the commencement of a rival frog-jump in 2007, is still going strong. The record for the longest jump has been held since 1986 by Lee Giudici, whose champion frog Rosie the Ribiter managed 6.55 m. There is a $5,000 prize awaiting the person whose frog can ever beat this distance.

If one had to choose a single word that encapsulates the comic appeal of frogs, it would undoubtedly be 'hapless'. And the frog that best performs the role is Kenneth Grahame's Mr Toad, of the novel, *The Wind in the Willows* (1908). Although the word 'hapless' only occurs twice in the text, it is forever associated with the impulsive and vainglorious batrachian, cruising for one of his numerous falls just like Aesop's exploding frog. Fearing for his arrest after stealing a motor car, Toad utters his memorable lament:

The Country Diversion of Leap-Frog.

Another popular recreation of batrachian locomotion: *The Country Diversion of Leap-frog*, etching after Hayman, *c.* 1743.

'A luckless bull-frog lost his voice while talking in his sleep, and now he'll never fish it out – his voice it is so deep.' A version of the perennially unfortunate batrachian from *Harper's Round Table*, 1896.

> O, what a fool I have been! What did I want to go strutting about the country for, singing conceited songs . . . instead of hiding till nightfall and slipping home quietly by back ways! O hapless Toad! O ill-fated animal!

'Hapless' is funny because it implies that some grand, malevolent scheme of fortune is to blame, whereas in fact Toad's (relatively trivial) adversities arise entirely through defects in his own character: from his frogness, in fact. The critic Seth Lerer points out that Toad's words echo Milton's in *Paradise Lost*: 'O much deceiv'd, much failing, hapless Eve', again highlighting the preposterousness of Toad's self-regard.[2]

Mr Toad shares his overweening character with the hero of Beatrix Potter's *The Tale of Mr Jeremy Fisher* (1906). At the beginning, we are told that Jeremy can get away with what children generally cannot; he 'liked getting his feet wet' but 'nobody ever scolded him'. But, as fabular frogs are inclined to do, Mr Fisher over-reaches himself – in his case by going out to catch fish. Potter, as a keen naturalist, would have known that fish form no part of the common frog's diet; *Rana temporaria* sticks to invertebrates such as insects, slugs and worms. Mr Fisher adds conspicuous consumption to his sins; he plans to invite his two important-sounding acquaintances to dinner, but only if he catches at least five of the fish. This is the opposite of feeding the 5,000; here, only an excess of catering will do.

As a child, I remember being vaguely but unpleasantly disconcerted by Mr Fisher's dinky, white-clad feet. Now I realize that they lack webs; however, their insertion into galoshes forms an important part of the tale, for it is only due to proper rain-wear that Fisher escapes the trout that swallows him. Disliking the taste of his macintosh, the trout spits him back out. The fish does, however, swallow Fisher's galoshes, and for a few pages the frog displays naturalistic feet (although interestingly these are often modestly concealed in Potter's illustrations by water or foliage). When Fisher's friends arrive at the end of the book, the feet are once again tucked away inside spats and improbably tiny shoes. Potter finishes the tale with Fisher sharing a meal of insects with the tortoise and the newt: 'roasted grasshopper with lady-bird sauce; which frogs consider a beautiful treat; but *I* think it must have been nasty!' Jeremy Fisher has (just about) learned his place; he is permitted to have fun and be free so long as he obeys certain rules; he must wear galoshes and raincoat and must not aspire to inappropriate dining. His pictures summon up the image of a butler, and he may be unconsciously based in part upon Lewis Carroll's frog footman. His frogness is strictly disciplined within a particular framework of class and childhood.

Arnold Lobel's delightful Frog and Toad books span the 1970s, but with their poignant humour and characterization they recollect Kenneth Grahame's gentler touch. 'One day in summer, Frog was not feeling well', begins one:

Queen Alice conversing with an old and comic frog. Wood engraving after Tenniel's drawings for *Through the Looking Glass* (1872).

'Toad said, 'Frog, you are looking quite green.'

'But I always look green,' said Frog. 'I am a frog.'[3]

The stories are whimsical but never cloying, and have something of a Zen-like quality to them. Toad is a slightly more complex character, more given to grumpiness and melancholy, but also more resourceful than Frog. Frog's blitheness, however, often carries the day more successfully than Toad's deliberation.

'A Swim' demonstrates Lobel's straight-edged technique. Frog and Toad go for a swim, and Toad insists on wearing his bathing suit. He makes Frog promise not to look at him until he is in the water: 'because I look funny in my bathing suit', he explains. By the time they are ready to get back out, a curious crowd has gathered to see Toad, contrarily attracted by Frog's requests that they should go away and not look at his friend:

'If Toad looks funny in his bathing suit,' said the snake,
  'then I, for one, want to see him.'
'Me too,' said a field mouse.
'I have not seen anything funny for a long time.'[4]

Arnold Lobel's delightful (but inevitably comic) Frog and Toad.

Lobel avoids the clichéd children's book ending, whereby Toad's bathing suit somehow becomes invaluable, or the creatures learn that laughter at others' expense is wrong. Instead, it all turns out just as Toad predicted when he eventually starts to feel the cold and is obliged to emerge from the water:

> The tortoise laughed.
> The lizards laughed.
> The snake laughed.
> The field mouse laughed,
>   and Frog laughed.
> 'What are you laughing at, Frog?' said Toad.
> 'I am laughing at you, Toad,' said Frog, 'Because you do
>   look funny in your bathing suit.'
> 'Of course I do,' said Toad. Then he picked up his clothes
>   and went home.[5]

Somehow, Toad's dignified response maintains the innocence of the laughter; the resolution denies a too-neat justice, but also keeps the world clean of cruelty. Frog and Toad are funny, but never diminished by Lobel.

Meanwhile, frogs have also been much in evidence in film, TV and Internet media. A frog named Flip was the hero of the first ever colour sound cartoon, *Fiddlesticks* (1930). The animators never quite seemed sure how to render a frog in cartoon form, having a particular problem with whether or not shoulders (and teeth) should be present. His character in earlier cartoons is similarly vague, and in *Fiddlesticks* his actions were confined to generalized capering. In successive films, Flip became less and less frog-like, and his character became a little more defined as a down-and-out, doing such unheroic things as spying on a woman in the shower and taking opium. In 1933, he disappeared

The apparently 'juvenile' element of the frog's brand-image did not dissuade Budweiser from using it to advertise their beer in a popular campaign of the 1990s.

altogether, but some twenty years later another singing and dancing frog took his place in the cartoon world. Michigan J. Frog debuted in 1955, in the Looney Tunes cartoon *One Froggy Evening* (described by Steven Spielberg as 'the Citizen Kane of animated film'). Michigan switches the classic frog joke into the human realm; in this tale it is a man that is haplessly ambitious. Discovering the remarkable performing frog, he plans to make his fortune out of showing him. But the frog remains resolutely silent when anyone else is present, and so his master's greed and hubris are punished. Despite remaining off-screen for 40 years, Michigan was revived as the mascot of the WB Television Network in 1995, only to be retired a decade later for giving an overly juvenile edge to the brand.

The year 1955 was also the year that Jim Henson's Kermit the Frog made his first appearance. Henson stitched the prototype

Arguably the most famous frog ever: Jim Henson's Kermit (b. 1955).

from his mother's overcoat and two ping-pong balls; at first he was indeterminately herpetological, and only over a decade or more did he gradually metamorphose into something unambiguously froggish. In *Sesame Street*, Kermit shared something of Mr Toad's overweening ambition, a frustrated know-it-all constantly bothered by the antics all about him. In *The Muppet Show*, he kept order and steered skilfully clear of Miss Piggy's attentions. Of all Henson's puppets, Kermit appears to have been the creature closest to his maker's heart. Henson voiced Kermit, compared his lot in life to his own, and used him as the logo of his company. He retained control of the character after rights to the others were sold on. But despite Kermit's many positive attributes, only the cruellest parent would today choose the once-common name – now forever linked with the frog – for their son. Like his namesake, such a boy would most certainly find that 'it's not easy being green'.

The protagonist of *Frogger* was a hapless frog *par excellence*. This 1981 arcade game, which quickly became available for the earliest home computers, featured a frog that players had to navigate to safety across a multi-lane highway and a dangerous river.

Alas, real frogs and toads face the challenge of roads that lie between their elevated feeding zones and lower-lying breeding grounds. Occasionally – and notably in the UK – these have toad-crossings at particularly vulnerable points; elsewhere, toads have to be content with road signs warning of their presence. These unintentionally humorous (and, one suspects, ineffective) signs perfectly echo the poignant comic appeal of *Frogger*.

It is a horrible irony that frogs are, in terms of ecological threat, amongst the most hapless of all animals today. Over the past 30 years, habitat destruction, pollution, collection, UV-B radiation, climate change and pandemics have all contributed to massive declines and extinctions of numerous species: a 'perfect storm' for the frog, according to many scientists. In 2004, it was estimated that more than 120 species had become extinct since the 1980s; today, that figure is likely to be even higher. Malcolm McCallum of Texas A&M University puts the current

A close view of a Wyoming toad (*Bufo baxteri* or *Anaxyrus baxteri*), victim of the 'perfect storm' that is leading to extinction for many anurans. The species suffered a sharp decline during the 1970s and has been extinct in the wild since 1991.

This *Woodland Still-life with a Frog* is an unusually early representation of a frog within its habitat – although its elements may be symbolic rather than naturalistic. (Johann-Adalbert Angermeyer, 1736, oil on copper.)

rate of frog extinction at an unimaginable 25,000–45,000 times the natural background level; others agree that over one-third of species are currently threatened. This figure was produced by over 500 scientists working together on the Global Amphibian Assessment in 2004, updated in 2006 and 2008.

Since 1989, frogs have commonly been described as 'biological indicators' of ecological health, a somewhat vague term

The Solomon Island leaf frog (*Ceratobatrachus guentheri*) seems to be a survivor of environmental degradation, flourishing in the ravaged forests of Papua New Guinea and its recent urban gardens.

that is generally taken to mean that their numbers are sensitive to habitat contamination in general, and also that they reflect population levels in other types of animals (so that if frogs decline, we can assume that mammals and trees have declined to a comparable degree).[6] Two reasons are commonly given for the frog's role as environmental bellwether: that it inhabits both water and land, so is exposed to a particularly wide range of environmental stresses; and that its absorbent skin makes it sensitive to any pollutants in its habitat. Pesticides, for example, have been implicated in frogs' compromised immune systems and reduced ability to breed – even sterility.[7] The British-based herpetologists Trevor Beebee and Richard Griffiths are cautious about the generalized notion of frogs as biological indicators, however, pointing out that some are actually 'tough as old boots' and able to take advantage of changed habitats.

The collection of frogs – by scientists and traders – has had a serious impact on frog numbers. Unusual or attractive species such as members of the Madagascan genus *Mantella* are particularly at risk, being taken in unsustainable numbers from

The Panamanian golden frog (*Atelopus zeteki*) is a critically endangered toad, now probably extinct in the wild. Only after it had been allowed to die out did the Panamanian government decide to enshrine it as a national symbol, commemorated annually.

the wild. These days, the understandable desire to buy and keep gem-like, colourful frogs can be harmlessly satisfied by the Apple app, *Pocket Frogs* (2010). This game successfully taps into many features of the urge to collect: aesthetic appeal, rarity, ownership, care, breeding – and perhaps showing off – and has proved a huge success. Alas, no such virtual alternative exists for the eating of frogs. The consumption of frogs poses at least a two-fold threat to their continued existence; firstly by their straightforward destruction for eating, and secondly by the introduction of edible or farmed species – notably bullfrogs – which out-compete or even predate upon native anurans.

Quite besides all these other problems – and by far the most immediate threat to frogs at the present time – is a disease known as chytridiomycosis, caused by the fungus *Batrachochytrium dendrobatidis* (Bd). Spores of Bd invade the skin of anurans, breaking down their cells to steal nutrients, and eventually producing spores which can either re-infect the host or spread to further victims. The skin of infected frogs is visibly damaged, and can no longer properly absorb water or oxygen. The animals become lethargic and unresponsive to environmental stress. Infected frogs are most easily spotted due to their odd sitting posture, with legs trailing helplessly out behind them rather than tucked under the body in a neat squat.

Unexplained groups of dead and dying frogs were first spotted in Queensland in 1993; five years later, Bd was identified as the cause of this mysterious disease. Since then, chytridiomycosis has devastated frog populations around the globe. Around 30 per cent of species have been affected to date; once Bd is present in a population, 80 per cent of individuals can be expected to be dead within a year. This is an average figure; sometimes the annihilation is total. Herpetologists are sometimes in the distressing and tragic position of describing new species from the dead specimens that they find; discovery and extinction bookend their descriptions. The Australian researcher

This frog pendant, 3rd–8th century CE from modern-day Peru, perhaps reflects modern the urge to collect and own perfect little frogs – whether living or as App 'pocket frogs'.

The Caribbean giant ditch frog or mountain chicken frog (*Leptodactylus fallax*) – one of the world's largest species – has been brought to the point of extinction partly by human consumption.

179

Lee Berger, who along with colleagues discovered the role of ʙd in chytridiomycosis, states that the disease is producing 'the most spectacular loss of vertebrate biodiversity due to disease in recorded history'. Other herpetologists simply report weeping as they return to their study pools and find them empty.

Is ʙd a new pathogen, or is it an old one that has recently increased its virulence? Or is the problem that it has spread beyond an original host population that had good immunity, and into an unprotected wider world? *Xenopus laevis*, the African clawed frog, is one species that can be infected by ʙd but has low morbidity. Preserved specimens from the early twentieth century, held in European laboratories, have been tested for the disease and one from 1938 was found to be infected. This has prompted suspicion that the global trade in *X. laevis* for pregnancy testing helped to spread the fungus far and wide. There is a similar concern over the American bullfrog, which also has high resistance to ʙd and also has been introduced around the globe – for eating, in this case. The spores of ʙd can travel only very short distances – 1–2 cm – and so it seems likely that the

A frog suffering from chytridiomycosis.

A Chinese pharmacist displays her collection of dried frogs and lizards. Trade in biological materials such as these poses a direct threat to some species, and moreover increases the global transmission of infective agents such as Bd.

unnatural proximity of frogs in human keeping has had a significant role to play in the spread of the disease. Other possible human factors to blame for the pandemic include the use of pesticides that further reduce the resistance of anurans to Bd, and changed climates that favour the fungus more than previously.

The discipline of herpetology is today more focused on conservation than perhaps any other animal specialism. The First World Congress of Herpetology (1989) in Canterbury, UK, was a turning point; scientists compared notes and realized that all of them were seeing major declines in the species they were studying. From then on, anxiety about survival became key to the discipline. Today, herpetologists are understandably concentrating most of their resources on combating chytridiomycosis, but with little success to date. There has been some suggestion that coating frogs' skin with a certain bacterium will afford protection from the disease; painstaking treatments with anti-fungal agents have also had some positive results. Neither of these ideas, however, seems like a realistic treatment for wild populations in the near future. Meanwhile, a programme of breeding in captivity has begun, a Noah's ark approach to the desperately sad possibility that many wild populations might simply disappear. A rather sci-fi backstop, the Amphibian Ark Biobanking Advisory Committee was formed in 2008. This body explores strategies for cryopreserving cells from frogs and other Amphibia, in the hopes that they might one day be resurrected and re-released. As if the effects of chytridiomycosis were not depressing enough, some herpetologists warn that too much focus upon it will allow other issues such as deforestation and climate change – over which we might have more control – to continue apace. Scientists at the Amphibian Conservation Summit of 2005 worked out a five-year action plan to address all aspects of conservation, budgeted at $409 m.

This beautiful *Dendropsophus ebraccatus* illustrates the limited value of artificial conservation without agreement on ecosystem protection; it is impossible to breed in captivity. Thankfully the species is not yet endangered.

The best chance of mobilizing help on this kind of financial scale requires tapping in to some kind of popular concern and understanding of biodiversity issues. Rainforests seem as though they might be a good place to start. Rainforests have long been a focus of concern for biodiversity conservation, and in more recent years ecologists have also emphasized the value of these 'lungs of the planet' in regulating the Earth's climate. Rainforests are actually rather lacking in the large, charismatic species that are typically used to excite popular interest in biodiversity issues, but there are plenty of beautiful and unusual frogs to take their

place. Indeed, these have now come to stand for the plants and animals of the world's threatened tropical forests. The Rainforest Alliance (f. 1986) uses an image of a frog on its accreditation mark for responsibly produced goods, such as coffee. 'The little green frog is your assurance that goods and services are produced in a socially, economically and environmentally sustainable way', the Alliance explains on its website. At the time of writing (early 2011), it states that Mars Inc. has undertaken to earn the frog's seal of approval for their Galaxy chocolate bars in the short term, and for all their chocolate products by 2020.

This is a start, but it will take considerably more than bars of chocolate to protect the frog in its latest and most dangerous metamorphosis – into a creature of the warming world that it shares with humans. Each species that dies out is a grievous loss, for what Swammerdam wrote 350 years ago remains true to this day: 'There is a much greater number of miracles, and natural secrets in the Frog, than any one hath ever before thought of or discovered.'[8]

Timeline of the Frog

200 million years ago	c. 3000 BCE	405 BCE	c. 1st or 2nd century CE
Earliest confirmed modern frog lives in Argentina	The Egyptian goddess Heket is commemorated in frog figurines	Aristophanes writes *The Frogs*	The Mandukya Upanishad praises the spiritual lesson of the frog

Late 1770s	1812	1865	1869
Galvani begins his experiments on frogs' legs	The Brothers Grimm publish 'The Frog King' for the first time; it appears in English in 1823	'The Celebrated Jumping Frog of Calaveras County' is published by Mark Twain	Live frogs are placed in cold water and boiled slowly by Friedrich Goltz

1952	1960s	1961	1986
Robert Briggs and Thomas King create a tadpole with the nucleus from one egg and the outer matter from another	Bioprospectors begin to hunt out valuable pharmaceuticals in frogs	Soviet Union launches the first frogs into space	Rosie the Ribiter sets the world record for length of frog-jump at 6.55 m

c. 750	1115	1590	1777
Poet Li Bai describes the three-legged toad in the Moon	A magic frog mends a breached dyke in southern China and is rewarded with a temple dedicated to it	Forty witches attempt to kill the English King with a poison concocted from toads	Lazzaro Spallanzani achieves the first-ever artificial fertilized organism using frogs

1908	1930	1935	1950s
Auguste Escoffier launches the frog as *haute cuisine* for the English by sneaking it into the Prince of Wales's banquet	*Xenopus laevis* is introduced to Europe as breeding colonies for research; Flip the Frog stars in the first-ever colour sound cartoon	*Bufo marinus* is introduced to Australia	National People's Congress of China encourages women to swallow tadpoles as contraception

1990s	2004	2009
Toad smoking becomes fashionable; Queensland authorities ban possession of toad slime	Global Amphibian Assessment estimates that 120 of *c.* 6,000 frog species have become extinct since the 1980s; 32 per cent of frog species are in danger of extinction	Disney makes 'The Frog King' into a film – *The Princess and the Frog*

References

INTRODUCTION

1 Beverley F. Bell, 'When Is an Animal, Not an Animal?', *Journal of Biological Education*, XV (1981), pp. 213–18.

2 C. H. Brown, 'Folk Zoological Life-Forms: Their Universality and Growth', *American Anthropologist*, LXXXI (1979), pp. 791–817.

3 Ralph N. H. Bulmer and M. J. Tyler, 'Karam Classification of Frogs', *Journal of the Polynesian Society*, LXXVII (1968), pp. 333–85; Peter D. Dwyer and David C. Hyndman, '"Frog" and "Lizard": Additional Life-Forms from Papua New Guinea', *American Anthropologist*, LXXXV (1983), pp. 890–96.

4 Edward Topsell, *The History of Serpents; Or, the Second Book of Living Creatures*, appended to *The History of Four-Footed Beasts* (London, 1658), p. 597.

5 Topsell, *History of Serpents*, p. 726. The early Christian text *Physiologus* (*c.* 2nd century CE) appears to be the sole exception to this moral ordering of frogs and toads. Its author compares the 'frog of the dry place' with 'fine abstinent men', and the water frogs with those driven by their desires. Michael J. Curley, trans., *Physiologus: A Medieval Book of Nature Lore* (Austin, TX, and London, 1979), pp. 60–61.

6 Ralph N. H. Bulmer and Michael J. Tyler, 'Karam Classification of Frogs', *Journal of the Polynesian Society*, LXXVII (1968), pp. 333–85.

7 Kenneth R. Porter gives an overview of his discipline's history and key publications in the introduction to *Herpetology* (Philadelphia, London and Toronto, 1972).

8 Ernest Jones, *Essays in Applied Psychoanalysis* (London, 1951), vol. II, p. 94.

1 JUST A KISS

1 R. P. Chamakura, 'Bufotenine – A Hallucinogen in Ancient Snuff Powders of South America and a Drug of Abuse on the Streets of New York City', *Forensic Science Review*, VI (1994), pp. 1–18.
2 John [Jan] Swammerdam, *The Book of Nature, or, The History of Insects* (London, 1758), part II, p. 105.
3 See Jennifer Rampling, 'Establishing the Canon: George Ripley and His Alchemical Sources', *Ambix*, LV (2008), pp. 189–208. The source on which I have drawn here is Rampling's unpublished PhD thesis, University of Cambridge (2009).
4 Personal communication.
5 Carl Jung, *Psychology and Alchemy* (London, 1968), p. 327.
6 J. F. Campbell, *Popular Tales of the West Highlands: Orally Collected* (Edinburgh, 1860), vol. II, no. 33, pp. 130–32.
7 H. Parker, *Village Folk Tales of Ceylon* [1910] (Whitefish, MT, 2003), vol. I, pp. 67–72.
8 William Elliot Griffis, *The Unmannerly Tiger, and Other Korean Tales* (New York, 1911), pp. 112–25.
9 *Folk Tales from China*, 3rd series (Peking, 1958), pp. 74–82.
10 Jack Zipes, *The Brothers Grimm: From Enchanted Forests to the Modern World* (New York and London, 1988), p. 15.
11 James M. McGlathery, *Grimms' Fairy Tales: A History of Criticism on a Popular Classic* (Columbia, SC, 1993), p. 63.
12 Ernest Jones, *Essays in Applied Psycho-Analysis* (London, 1951), vol. II, p. 16.
13 McGlathery, *Grimms' Fairy Tales*, p. 62.
14 Bruno Bettelheim, *The Uses of Enchantment: The Meanings and Importance of Fairy Tales* (London and New York, 1991), p. 283.
15 Marina Warner, *From the Beast to the Blonde: On Fairy Tales and Their Tellers* (London, 1995), pp. 288–90.

16 Geoff Dench, *The Frog, The Prince, and the Problem of Men* (London, 1994), p. 251.

17 Jack Zipes, 'The Struggle for the Grimms' Throne: The Legacy of the Grimms' Tales in the FRG and GDR since 1945', in *The Reception of Grimms' Fairy Tales: Responses, Reactions, Revisions*, ed. Donald Haase (Detroit, MI, 1993), pp. 167–206; p. 190.

2 WARTS AND ALL

1 Translated in Kenneth R. Porter, *Herpetology* (Philadelphia, London and Toronto, 1972), p. 2.

2 Lazzaro Spallanzani, *Dissertations Relative to the Natural History of Animals and Vegetables* [1780] (London, 1789), vol. II, p. 50.

3 Michael Maierus, *Atalanta Fugiens* (Oppenheim, 1617), 5th discourse. Topsell in his *History of Serpents* gives the story as concerning a monk, and originating from Erasmus; the toad requires biting three times.

4 Edward Newman, *The Zoologist: A Popular Miscellany of Natural History*, X (London, 1852), p. 3,658.

5 Deborah Willis, *Malevolent Nurture: Witch-hunting and Maternal Power in Early Modern England* (Ithaca, NY, 1995), p. 126. In purely practical terms, they would not have succeeded.

6 Thomas Wright, *Narratives of Sorcery and Magic, from the Most Authentic Sources* (London, 1851), p. 308.

7 Cathy Gere, 'William Harvey's Weak Experiment: The Archaeology of an Anecdote', *History Workshop Journal*, LI (2001), pp. 19–36.

8 Edward A. Armstrong, *The Folklore of Birds: An Enquiry into the Origin and Distribution of Some Magico-Religious Traditions*, 2nd edn (New York, 1970), pp. 192–5.

9 Heinrich Kramer and Jacob Sprenger, *Malleus Maleficarum: Or, The Hammer of Witches* (www.forgottenbooks.org, 2008), pp. 198–201.

10 Kathleen Cohen, *Metamorphosis of a Death Symbol: The Transi Tomb in the Late Middle Ages and the Renaissance* (Berkeley, CA, 1973).

11 Sophie Page, 'Good Creation and Demonic Illusions: The Medieval Universe of Creatures', in *A Cultural History of Animals in the Medieval Age*, ed. Brigitte Resl (Oxford and New York, 2007), pp. 27–58.

3 THEM, US AND FROGS

1 Richard Wassersug, 'On the Comparative Palatability of Some Dry-season Tadpoles from Costa Rica', *American Midland Naturalist*, LXXXVI (1971), pp. 101–9.
2 Wolfram Eberhard, *The Local Cultures of South and East China* (Leiden, 1968), pp. 202–3.
3 Anonymous, 'Frog-Eating', *The Journal of American Folklore*, XV (1902), p. 190. Edgar Thurston and K. Rangachari, *Castes and Tribes of Southern India* (Madras, 1909), vol. VII.
4 John Claudius Loudon, *An Encyclopedia of Agriculture*, vol. II, p. 1,057.
5 William B. Jerrold, ed., *The Epicure's Year Book and Table Companion for 1869* (London, 1869), p. 167 and Jerrold, ed., *The Epicure's . . . 1868* (London, 1868), pp. 158 and 195–6.
6 Marie Antonin Carême and Armand Plumerey, *L'Art de la cuisine française au dix-neuvième siècle*, vol. V (Paris, 2005), pp. 255–9.
7 Kenneth James, *Escoffier: The King of Chefs* (London, 2002), pp. 135–54.
8 Shane Mitchell, 'Wild and Refined', *Saveur*, 128 (2010). At www.saveur.com.
9 UN comtrade, at http://comtrade.un.org.
10 Umberto Eco, *On Ugliness*, trans. Alistair McEwen (London, 2007), p. 19.
11 Edward Bartlett, *Wild Animals in Captivity* (London, 1899), pp. 200–1.
12 The following is drawn from Michael Randall, 'On the Evolution of Toads in the French Renaissance', *Renaissance Quarterly*, 57 (2004), pp. 126–64.
13 David Bindman, 'How the French Became Frogs: English

Caricature and Stereotypes of Nations', in *The European Print and Cultural Transfer in the Eighteenth and Nineteenth Centuries*, ed. Philippe Kaenel and Rolf Reichardt (Zürich, 2007), pp. 423–36. The whole of the section on Dutch and French caricature is drawn from Bindman's research.

14 Philippe Hecquet, *Traité des dispenses du carême* (Paris, 1709), pp. 164–5.

15 Bindman, 'How the French Became Frogs'.

16 Gilbert Abbott A'Beckett and John Leech, *The Comic History of England* (London, 1847), p. 116.

17 Tim Low, *Feral Future: The Untold Story of Australia's Exotic Invaders* (Chicago, IL, 2002), pp. 46–54.

4 UNDER THE KNIFE

 1 High Field Magnet Laboratory, Radboud University Nijmegen, 'The Frog that Learned to Fly', at www.ru.nl.

 2 *The Bible of Nature* was completed in manuscript form shortly before Swammerdam's death but was not published until 1737 in Dutch and 1758 in English, for which its title was translated as *The Book of Nature*.

 3 John [Jan] Swammerdam, *The Book of Nature, or, The History of Insects* (London, 1758), part II, p. 135.

 4 Ibid., part II, p. 111.

 5 *The European Magazine, and London Review*, LXIX (1816), p. 214.

 6 Robert Townson, *Tracts and Observations in Natural History and Physiology* (London, 1799), p. 115.

 7 Laura Otis, *Müller's Lab* (Oxford and New York, 2007).

 8 William Thompson Sedgwick, 'On Variations of Reflex Excitability in the Frog, Induced by Changes of Temperature', in *Studies from the Biological Laboratory*, vol. II, ed. Newell Martin (Baltimore, MD, 1883), pp. 385–410; 388–9.

 9 Sedgwick, 'On Variations of Reflex Excitability in the Frog', p. 386.

10 E. W. Scripture, *The New Psychology* (London, 1897), pp. 300–1.

11 Fast Company, 'Next Time, What Say We Boil a Consultant', *Fast*

Company, 31 October 1995, at www.fastcompany.com.

12 Animal Aid, 'Endangered Frogs – the Vivisection Connection'
    (posted 2008), at www.animalaid.org.uk.

5 EVOLUTION ON FAST-FORWARD

1 Robert Chambers, *Vestiges of the Natural History of Creation*
   (London, 1844), pp. 210–11.

2 Ernst Haeckel, *The History of Creation* [1868] (New York, 1880),
   vol. I, p. 294.

3 Haeckel, *History of Creation*, vol. I, pp. 310–11.

4 Mikhail Bulgakov, *The Fatal Eggs* (London, 2005), p. 17.

5 For the story of Russian and Soviet Darwinism, see Mark B. Adams,
   'Sergei Chetverikov, the Kol'tsov Institute, and Evolutionary
   Biology', in *The Evolutionary Synthesis: Perspectives on the
   Unification of Biology*, ed. Ernst Mayr and William B. Provine
   (Cambridge, MA, 1988), pp. 242–78.

6 This account of the history of *Xenopus laevis* is taken from John
   B. Gurdon and Nick Hopwood, 'The Introduction of *Xenopus
   laevis* into Developmental Biology: Of Empire, Pregnancy Testing
   and Ribosomal Genes', *International Journal of Developmental
   Biology*, XLIV (2000), pp. 43–50.

7 Bertha Chapman Cady and Vernon Mosher Cady, *The Way Life
   Begins: An Introduction to Sex Education* [1917], at
   Generalbooks.net (accessed 2010), p. 15.

8 Stephen Jay Gould, *Ontogeny and Phylogeny* (Cambridge, MA,
   1977), p. 1.

9 Personal communication.

6 OF FROGS AND FRUITFULNESS

1 Edward Newman, *The Zoologist: A Popular Miscellany of Natural
   History*, X (London, 1852), p. 3316.

2 George Orwell, 'Some Thoughts on the Common Toad', *Tribune*
   (1946).

3 See Sulochana R. Asirvatham et al., eds, *Between Magic and Religion: Interdisciplinary Studies in Ancient Mediterranean Religion and Society* (Lanham, MD, 2001), pp. 181–6.

4 Trevor Beebee and Richard Griffiths, *Amphibians and Reptiles: A Natural History of the British Herpetofauna* (London, 2000), p. 21.

5 Leo A. Orleans, 'Birth Control: Reversal or Postponement?', *The China Quarterly*, III (1960), pp. 59–70; p. 67.

6 Edward Polehampton, *Gallery of Nature and Art* (London, 1821), vol. V, p. 561.

7 Franc Johnson Newcomb, *Navaho Folk Tales* (Albuquerque, NM, 1990) pp. 151–61.

8 Julian B. Carter, 'Birds, Bees, and Venereal Disease: Toward an Intellectual History of Sex Education', *Journal of the History of Sexuality*, X (2001), pp. 213–49.

9 Mary Field, dir., *The Mystery of Marriage* (UK, 1932).

10 Red Squirrel [Cyril Bibby], 'The Story of Mr and Mrs Frog', *New Pioneer* (August 1939), pp. 118–19.

11 Lazzaro Spallanzani, *Dissertations Relative to the Natural History of Animals and Vegetables* (London, 1789), vol. II.

12 Ibid., vol. II, pp. 114–18.

13 Lazzaro Spallanzani, *An Essay on Animal Reproductions* (London, 1769), p. 43. Spallanzani dates his discovery to 1767 in *Dissertations*, vol. II, p. 144.

14 Spallanzani, *Dissertations*, vol. II, pp. 42–3.

15 Wolfram Eberhard, *The Local Cultures of South and East China* (Leiden, 1968), pp. 155 and 159.

16 E.T.C. Werner, *A Dictionary of Chinese Mythology* (New York, 1961); Werner, *Myths and Legends of China* (New York, 1976), pp. 125–6 and 128.

17 Charles Alfred Speed Williams, *Outlines of Chinese Symbolism and Art Motives* [1941] (New York, 1976), p. 403. However, like other sources, Williams states that 'Liu Hai sporting with the toad' is a figure of good luck.

18 Patricia Bjaaland Welch, *Chinese Art: A Guide to Motifs and Visual Imagery* (North Clarendon, VT, 2008), p. 106.

1   Michael J. Tyler et al., 'How Frogs and Humans Interact:
    Influences beyond Habitat Destruction, Epidemics and Global
    Warming', *Applied Herpetology*, IV (2007), pp. 1–18.
2   Kenneth Grahame, *The Wind in the Willows: An Annotated Edition*,
    ed. Seth Lerer (Cambridge, MA, 2009), p. 216.
3   Arnold Lobel, *Frog and Toad Are Friends* [1970] (Surrey, 1978),
    p. 16.
4   Ibid., pp. 46–7.
5   Ibid., pp. 51–2.
6   Trevor Beebee and Richard Griffiths, 'The Amphibian Decline
    Crisis: A Watershed for Conservation Biology?', *Biological
    Conservation*, CXXV (2005), pp. 271–85.
7   University of California, 'Pesticide Atrazine Can Turn Male Frogs
    into Females', (1 March 2010), at www.universityofcalifornia.edu.
8   John [Jan] Swammerdam, *The Book of Nature* (London, 1758), part
    II, p. 105.

Select Bibliography

Bárta, Miroslav, 'The Title "Priest of Heket" in the Egyptian Old Kingdom', *Journal of Near Eastern Studies*, LVIII (1999), pp. 107–16

Beebee, Trevor J. C., and Richard A. Griffiths, 'The Amphibian Decline Crisis: A Watershed for Conservation Biology?', *Biological Conservation*, CXXV (2005), pp. 271–85

Beetschen, Jean-Claude, 'How Did Urodele Embryos Come into Prominence as a Model System?', *International Journal of Developmental Biology*, XL (1996), pp. 629–36

Boll, Valerie, *Autour du Couple Ambigu Crapaud-Grenouille: Recherches Ethnozoologiques* (Paris, 2000)

Bowler, Peter, 'Fins and Limbs and Fins into Limbs: The Historical Context, 1840–1940', in *Fins into Limbs: Evolution, Development, and Transformation*, ed. Brian Keith Hall (Chicago, IL, 2007), pp. 7–14

Bulmer, Ralph N. H., and Michael J. Tyler, 'Karam Classification of Frogs', *Journal of the Polynesian Society*, LXXVII (1968), pp. 333–85

Cobb, Matthew, *The Egg and Sperm Race: The Seventeenth-century Scientists Who Unlocked the Secrets of Sex and Growth* (London, 2006)

DeGraaff, Robert M., *The Book of the Toad: A Natural and Magical History of Toad-Human Relations* (Rochester, VT, 1991)

Dubois, Alain, 'The Higher Nomenclature of Recent Amphibians', *Alytes*, XXII (2004), pp. 1–14

Eberhard, Wolfram, *The Local Cultures of South and East China* (Leiden, 1968)

Erspamer, Vittorio, 'Bioactive Secretions of the Amphibian
   Integument', in *Amphibian Biology*, vol. 1: *The Integument*, ed.
   H. Heatwole and G. T. Barthalmus (Chipping Norton, NSW, 1994)

Gascon, Claude, et al., eds, *Amphibian Conservation Action Plan.*
   Proceedings of the IUCN/SSC Amphibian Conservation Summit 2005
   (Gland, Switzerland, 2007)

Gere, Cathy, 'William Harvey's Weak Experiment: The Archaeology
   of an Anecdote', *History Workshop Journal*, LI (2001), pp. 19–36

Gilbert, Scott F., ed., *A Conceptual History of Modern Embryology*
   (Baltimore, MD, and London, 1991); see especially chapters by
   Maienschein and Saha

Gliboff, Sander, '"Protoplasm . . . Is Soft Wax in Our Hands": Paul
   Kammerer and the Art of Biological Transformation', *Endeavour*,
   XXIX (2005), pp. 162–7

Gould, Stephen Jay, *Ontogeny and Phylogeny* (Cambridge, MA, 1977)

Gurdon, John B., and Nick Hopwood, 'The Introduction of *Xenopus
   laevis* into Developmental Biology: Of Empire, Pregnancy Testing
   and Ribosomal Genes', *International Journal of Developmental
   Biology*, XLIV (2000), pp. 43–50

Hamburger, Jeffrey, 'Bosch's "Conjuror": An Attack on Magic and
   Sacramental Heresy', *Simiolus: Netherlands Quarterly for the History
   of Art*, XIV (1984), pp. 5–23

Holmes, Frederic L., 'The Old Martyr of Science: The Frog in
   Experimental Physiology', *Journal of the History of Biology*, XXVI
   (1993), pp. 311–28

Lewis, Mark, dir., *Cane Toads: An Unnatural History* (Australia, 1988);
   there is also a follow-up film, *Cane Toads: The Conquest* (2010)

Mattison, Chris, *Frogs and Toads* (London, 2011)

McDiarmid, Roy W., and Ronald Altig, *Tadpoles: The Biology of
   Anuran Larvae* (Chicago, IL, 1999)

Newton, Giles, 'Why the Frog?', in *The Human Genome* (on the
   Wellcome Trust website, http://genome.wellcome.ac.uk, 2004)

Nyhart, Lynn K., *Biology Takes Form: Animal Morphology and the
   German Universities, 1800–1900* (Chicago, IL, and London, 1995)

Otis, Laura, *Müller's Lab* (Oxford and New York, 2007)

Pera, Marcello, *The Ambiguous Frog: The Galvani-Volta Controversy on Animal Electricity*, trans. Jonathan Mandelbaum (Princeton, NJ, 1992)

Richards, Robert, *The Tragic Sense of Life: Ernst Haeckel and the Struggle over Evolutionary Thought* (Chicago, IL, and London, 2008)

Rosenhof, August Johann Rösel von, *Historia naturalis Ranarum nostratium* (Nuremburg, 1758), online at http://num-scd-ulp.u-stras-bg.fr

Sleigh, Charlotte, 'Plastic Body, Permanent Body: Czech Representations of Corporeality in the Early Twentieth Century', *Studies in History and Philosophy of Biological and Biomedical Sciences*, XL (2009), pp. 241–55

Swammerdam, John [Jan], *The Book of Nature, or, The History of Insects* (London, 1758), at http://digital.lib.usu.edu

Tyler, Michael J., et al., 'How Frogs and Humans Interact: Influences Beyond Habitat Destruction, Epidemics and Global Warming', *Applied Herpetology*, IV (2007), pp. 1–18

Wells, Kentwood D., *The Ecology and Behavior of Amphibians* (Chicago, IL, 2007)

Associations and Websites

Scientists who study frogs are members of herpetological associations, of which there are too many around the world to list. The Society for the Study of Amphibians and Reptiles (f. 1958; www.ssarherps. org) is the largest international herpetological society, a not-for-profit organization established to advance research, conservation and education concerning amphibians and reptiles. The Herpetologists' League (f. 1946; www.herpetologistsleague.org/en) is another major international organization, and the American Society of Ichthyologists and Herpetologists (f. *c.* 1913; www.asih.org) also has international reach. In Europe, the Societas Europaea Herpetologica (f. 1979; http://t-ad.net/ishbh) links up herpetologists including, in Great Britain, the British Herpetological Society (f. 1947; www.thebhs.org) and the Amphibian and Reptile Conservation trust (f. 2009; www.arc-trust. org).

Members of all these associations, and more, meet every three to five years at the World Congress of Herpetology (f. 1982; www.worldcon gressofherpetology.org). The International Society for the History and Bibliography of Herpetology (f. 1998; http://t-ad.net/ishbh) keeps track of the discipline and its publications.

The International Herpetological Society (http://international-herpeto logical-society.org) is a club for amateur breeders and keepers. Australia appears to be unique in having (at least) three amateur societies devoted specifically to anurans: the Frog and Tadpole Study Group of NSW, the Queensland Frog Society, and the Victorian Frog Group.

WEBSITES

AmphibiaWeb is an online system that provides access to information on amphibian declines, conservation, natural history and taxonomy. It is a very rich and frequently-updated source of knowledge about anurans, compiled at the University of California, Berkeley.
http://amphibiaweb.org

The Amphibian Specialist Group, supports a global web of partners aiming to achieve shared, strategic amphibian conservation goals, including a search for 'lost' species.
www.amphibians.org

The amphibians section of the IUCN Red List is dedicated to amphibian species that are currently highly threatened.
http://www.iucnredlist.org

The Biodiversity Heritage Library has photographic online versions of many original works mentioned in *Frog*. These include books by Charles Darwin, Richard Owen, Wilhelm Roux (in German), Ernst Haeckel (German and English), Lazzaro Spallanzani (English) and many more.
www.biodiversitylibrary.org

D. L. Ashliman, 'Frog Kings', (last updated 2008), has fourteen different versions of the Frog King tale from around the world, along with further links.
www.pitt.edu/~dash/frog.html#taylor

The Whole Frog Project is a rich and detailed virtual frog dissection resource.
http://froggy.lbl.gov

The Amphibian Specialist Group, supports a global web of partners aiming to achieve shared, strategic amphibian conservation goals, including a search for 'lost' species.
www.amphibians.org

The amphibians section of the IUCN Red List is dedicated to amphibian species that are currently highly threatened.
http://www.iucnredlist.org

The Biodiversity Heritage Library has photographic online versions of many original works mentioned in *Frog*. These include books by Charles Darwin, Richard Owen, Wilhelm Roux (in German), Ernst Haeckel (German and English), Lazzaro Spallanzani (English) and many more.
www.biodiversitylibrary.org

D. L. Ashliman, 'Frog Kings', (last updated 2008), has fourteen different versions of the Frog King tale from around the world, along with further links.
www.pitt.edu/~dash/frog.html#taylor

The Whole Frog Project is a rich and detailed virtual frog dissection resource.
http://froggy.lbl.gov

Acknowledgements

I am grateful to the following people for generously sharing their expertise and contributing gems of anuran knowledge:

Alixe Bovey, Matthew Cobb, Stefan Goebel, Richard Griffiths, Lesley Hall, Diane Heath, Mubariz Hussain, Dunstan Lowe, Sophie Page, Julie Peakman, Neil Pemberton, Christopher Plumb, Jenny Rampling, Victoria Resnick, John-Paul Riordan, Janine Rogers, Gill Sinclair, Paul Sleigh, Crosbie Smith, Nick Thurston, Richard Wassersug.

Thank you most especially to Alice White, who did such a wonderful job researching and obtaining the pictures for *Frog*.

Photo Acknowledgements

The author and the publishers wish to express their thanks to the below sources of illustrative material and/or permission to reproduce it.

Andrey: p. 43; The Art Institute of Chicago: p. 146 bottom (Wirt D. Walker Fund Income 1969.792); Steven Barker: p. 142; Sergio Barbierei: p. 152; Forrest Brem. From open access creative commons article: Gewin V (2008) Riders of aModern-Day Ark. *PLoS Biol* 6(1): e24.doi: 10.1371/journal.pbio.0060024: p. 180; British Cartoon Archive, University of Kent: p. 89; British Library, London: pp. 62, 158; © The Trustees of the British Museum: pp. 73, 86, 163, 164, 167; Jeremy Brooks (jeremy brooks.net): p. 173; Canterbury Cathedral Archives: p. 99; Phil Carter: p. 166; Cleveland Museum of Art, Ohio: pp. 145 (Andrew R. and Martha Holden Jennings Fund 1976.5), 179 top right (Gift of W. J. Gordon 1955.375); © Depositphotos: p. 156 (Yuliya Krzhevka); Fine Arts Museums of San Francisco: p. 35; Christian Fisher: p. 130; Froggydarb: pp. 18, 33; Getty Images: pp. 22 right, 26, 175; Brian Gratwicke: pp. 177, 178; R. A. Griffiths: p. 131; Peter Halasz: p. 136; High Field Magnet Laboratory, Radboud University, Nijmegen, The Netherlands: p. 97; Used with permission of HarperCollins Publishers: p. 167; Jeremy Hubert: p. 84; Chris Irie: p. 144; Istockphoto: p. 6 (Paul Tessier); © Estate Martin Kippenberger, Galerie Gisela Capitain, Cologne: p. 114; Christoph Leeb: p. 101; Library of Congress: pp. 103, 168; LiquidGhoul: p. 22 left; The Lord of the Allaurs: p. 24; NASA: p. 98; National Library of Medicine, Bethesda, Maryland: p. 181; National Library of the Netherlands: p. 65; Minneapolis College of Art and Design Collection: p. 42; The

Minneapolis Institute of Arts Collection: p. 117 (The Ethel Morrison van Derlip Fund 66.25.171); Des Musées de Strasbourg: p. 71; Princeton University Library: p. 37; Rex Features: pp. 16 top (Design Pics Inc), 23 (Chris Martin Bahr), 53 (c. Walt Disney/Everett/Rex Features), 78 (MonkeyBusiness Images), 79 (Bernard Caselein/Nature Picture Library), 93 (MonkeyBusiness Images); Professor David S. Richard, Susquehanna University: p. 112; Science Photo Library: pp. 104 (Sheila Terry), 137 (National Museum of Heath and Science); Dr Tony Shaw: p. 74; Courtesy of Special Collections, University of Houston Library: p. 9; Tnarg 12345: p. 15; University of California, San Diego: p. 146 top; Tim Vickers: p. 179 bottom; Kevin Walsh: p. 14; Warburg Institute, London: pp. 11, 34, 61, 69, 176; Wellcome Library, London: pp. 10, 64, 118; Andrea E Wills: p. 127; W-van: p. 16 bottom; Zoological Society of London: pp. 12, 19, 21, 27, 29, 32, 57, 113, 128, 141, 146, 154.

Index